SWEDENBORG'S
JOURNAL OF DREAMS
1743-1744

SWEDENBORG'S
JOURNAL OF DREAMS
1743-1744

Emanuel Swedenborg

Edited from the original Swedish
by *G. E. Klemming*

Translated into English, 1860,
by *J. J. G. Wilkinson*

Edited by *William Ross Woofenden*

With an Introduction
by *Wilson Van Dusen,*

Second Edition, 1989

Swedenborg Scientific Association
Bryn Athyn, PA

Swedenborg Society
London, England

Library of Congress Cataloging-in-Publication Data

Swedenborg, Emanuel, 1688-1772.

[Drömboken. English]

Swedenborg's journal of dreams, 1743-1744 / Emanuel Swedenborg; edited from the original Swedish by G.E. Klemming; translated into English 1860 by J.J.G. Wilkinson; edited by William Ross Woofenden; with an introduction by Wilson Van Dusen. — 2nd ed.

p. cm.

Translation of: Drömboken.

Includes bibliographical references.

ISBN 0-915221-67-5

1. Swedenborg, Emanuel, 1688-1772—Diaries. 2. Mystics—Sweden—Diaries—Early works to 1800. 3. Dreams—Early works to 1800.

I. Klemming, G. E. II. Woofenden, William Ross. III. Title. IV. Title: Journal of dreams, 1743-1744.

BX8712.D994   1989

289.4' 092—dc20

[B]   89-39612

British Library Cataloguing in Publication Data

Swedenborg, Emanuel, 1688-1772

Swedenborg's Journal of dreams 1743-1744. — 2nd ed.

1. Dreams — Biographies

I. Title II. Klemming, G. E. III. Woofenden, William Ross, 1921 - IV. Swedenborg Society V. Swedenborg's drommar, 1744. English

135.3092

ISBN 0-85448-109-5

To Lennart O. Alfelt

PREFACE TO THE SECOND EDITION

The first English edition of this version of Swedenborg's *Journal of Dreams*, published in 1977 by the Swedenborg Foundation, is out of print. It was apparently the decision of the editorial and publication board of the Foundation to regard their 1986 publication, *Swedenborg's Journal of Dreams, 1743-1744: Commentary by Wilson Van Dusen*, as a wholly adequate replacement for the 1977 edition.

There is reason to hold this view: Dr. Van Dusen's version does contain, as an integral part of his Chapter 2, the entire text of the original work. This chapter (pages 10-165) however, comprises not only Swedenborg's text but also Van Dusen's commentary, interspersed with the text. Not surprisingly, the commentary is often much longer than the passages referred to. Thus, in order for the reader to read just the words of Swedenborg, it is necessary to thumb through more than 150 larger-format pages in order to read what was contained seriatim in 90 smaller-format pages in the 1977 edition.

It should be noted that this observation is not to be construed as depreciating the value or significance of Van Dusen's valuable professional insights found in his comments. It is simply to note that the reader whose primary interest is in the original text is faced with some inconvenience if the only version available is the 1986 volume. On the other hand, for those seeking interpretive help in understanding the original text, Van Dusen's version will serve them well, and is commended to their attention.

Reference is made in the Preface to the 1977 edition (q.v.) to one of the shortcomings of the 1918 English edition of the *Journal of Dreams* translated and edited by C. Th. Odhner, namely his seemingly Victorian decision to translate certain passages into Latin rather than English. What was *not* mentioned was that Odhner had done extensive research concerning references by Swedenborg about people, contemporary events, etc., and had included these data in a number of footnotes. *Some* of this information was included in the 1977 edition, but most of it was not.

The primary change in this 1989 edition is the inclusion of most of Odhner's reference material in footnotes. In some cases, however, instead of including his lengthy biographical abstracts, the reader is referred to other books for the details. And in some instances, items included by Odhner that seem to be entirely conjectural in nature have been omitted.

Perhaps the most indefensible omission by the editor of the 1977 edition was his failure to give expression of thanks and due credit for the invaluable editorial assistance given to him by the late Lennart Alfelt. When the decision was made to publish the Wilkinson translation serially in *Studia Swedenborgiana*, the undersigned prevailed on his good friend, Mr. Alfelt, to draw on his expertise in

Swedish and to compare Wilkinson's version with
the original Swedish text. This he did, both cheerful-
ly and thoroughly, and the resulting text printed
first in *Studia* and later in the 1977 Swedenborg
Foundation edition, was greatly improved over the
original Wilkinson version, in large part because of
Mr. Alfelt's efforts. Belatedly, this editor here expres-
ses his profound thanks and indebtedness to this
remarkable servant of the Church.

William Ross Woofenden

Sharon, Massachusetts, 1989

PREFACE TO THE 1977 EDITION[1]

The Royal Library in Stockholm purchased in October 1858 the original manuscript that contains the principal contents of this little volume. It had previously long lain concealed in the possession of R. Scheringsson, Professor and Master in Västerås (not far from Stockholm), who died in 1849 at the age of 90. The manuscript continued hidden among his papers for nearly ten years more after his decease, and was ultimately offered for sale to the Royal Library. The handwritten document is contained in a common memorandum book in small octavo, bound in parchment after the fashion of the 17th Century, and provided with wrappers and pockets on both sides. At present the leaves number 69, but some leaves, probably not written on, have been torn out. Of those which remain, there is writing on only 54 sheets, or more exactly speaking, 104 pages. The first leaves are notes of a journey to The Hague in 1743, where Swedenborg went to superintend the printing of the first volume of *Regnum Animale* [the soul's kingdom], and to write the continuation of that work. The notes of travel are however soon brought to an end, and are

---

[1]Adapted in part from the Preface to the original 1859 Swedish edition of Swedenborgs Drömmar.

succeeded by accounts derived from the world of dream and vision, although among the latter there are also scattered notices of the external and actual life. "Embracing as they do the transition period in Swedenborg's life—the transition from the worldly to the spiritual—they are of great value in helping us form a judgment of his spiritual condition, which they show us to have been one of singular agitation and upheaval, enabling us to penetrate his state with deeper gaze than was previously possible. Nevertheless, the editor [G.E. Klemming] deals with the subject solely in the interest of literary history, and confines his office to the task of offering this document just as he found it. The thoughtful reader will easily form his own conclusions; and for the rest, we may be assured there will be no lack of commentators."

So wrote the editor who first published this work. In the original preface he went on to note the difficulties of "dealing with a piece of writing executed with so little care, and consequently often so dubious in its expressions and so difficult to read." His decision was to try to render it as exactly as possible, even to the italicizing of words underscored in the manuscript. He also employed the services of a distinguished reader of manuscripts, F. A. Dahlgren, who "with his usual penetration and ingenuity successfully guessed many of the words which were hard to decipher."

Gustaf Klemming, editor of the 1859 edition, was however an avowed enemy of Swedenborgianism as a religion, but was greatly interested in it as what *he* considered it to be, namely, a strange venture into the world of the occult.

The following year (1860), disturbed by Klemming's edition, a group of Swedenborgians published a second Swedish edition with a 24-page preface of "reflections on the lately discovered dreams of Swedenborg." Although unsigned, this preface was apparently written by a Lady Anna Frederika Ehrenborg. She had explained in the reflections that Swedenborg was passing through a personal crisis during the time he was hastily scribbling the contents of this journal. Her obvious intent was to help the reader to view the work with a better perspective. A third Swedish edition edited by Knut Barr appeared in Stockholm in 1924. It included a commentary on the *Journal* as well as a biographical sketch of Swedenborg. A fourth edition was published in 1952 by Wahlstrom & Widstrand, Stockholm, with Per Erik Wahlund as editor. A slightly revised fifth edition with a considerably enlarged body of notes was issued by the same publisher in 1964.

The first English translation—and to date the only complete English translation—is this present one of J. J. G. Wilkinson. This edition was first published serially in *Studia Swedenborgiana*, the occasional journal of the Swedenborg School of

Religion, 'Newton, Massachusetts, Volume I, 1974-75.

A pirated and abridged version of Wilkinson's translation, which claimed to be the work of a Baron Holmfeld of Denmark, appeared in "The Dawn," a London monthly, in 1861-1862. Later this version was reprinted in "The Crisis," a paper published at LaPorte, Indiana, in the 1860s. Dr. R. L. Tafel, in his three-volume *Documents Concerning Swedenborg* (London, 1875-77), methodically exposed the plagiaristic nature of Holmfeld's purported new translation. In the course of his exposé, Tafel was moved to translate and print (as Document 209) a large part of the contents of the 1743-44 journal. However, he omitted most of the entries before March 24, 1744, and also several scattered sections which he apparently felt were too explicit or indelicate for the average reader.

Although Tafel, following Swedenborg's usual practice of numbering paragraphs, did insert such numbers in his abridged version, the next English translator found he had to renumber the work to allow for Tafel's omissions. This version, edited by Carl Theophilus Odhner (Bryn Athyn, Pennsylvania, 1918), has become the standard for references to this work among English readers. One major drawback for scholars of this edition is that although Odhner did indeed include the sexually explicit passages Tafel omitted, he chose to translate them not into English but into Latin. Thus the present version, that of Wilkinson edited to conform to contemporary English by the undersigned, remains the only extant complete version in English. The paragraph numbers used in this edition agree with those used by Odhner.

William Ross Woofenden

Sharon, Massachusetts, 1976

SWEDENBORG'S JOURNEY WITHIN

by Wilson Van Dusen

It is a strange experience to be handed someone's *Journal of Dreams*. It is a compliment to be entrusted with the intimate secrets of someone's life. But it is an ambiguous situation, for these intimate secrets are written in a foreign and barely intelligible language. The purpose of this introduction is to help make this particular account more intelligible.

To begin with, this *Journal of Dreams* was obviously not intended for publication. We are privileged to see a very personal journal, sometimes scratched out in the middle of the night after a dream or vision. Because Swedenborg did not actually invite us to see this, we should treat this material with some respect. We are privileged to see here what is probably the oldest and longest series of dreams available in any language. For those who really want to understand spiritual development we could not have had a more fortuitous kind of material. The *Journal* was written just when Swedenborg, the scientist, was changing to become the religious seer. These dreams show the development leading to his later experience of heaven and hell. Swedenborg sought to meet God within, and these dreams are a glimpse into the dialogue of changes in this meeting. While he was given his highest wish, the Divine response also led him into personal changes that would aid him to receive the Divine.

What is a dream? Those who have not looked closely consider it to be some sort of useless fancy that spins itself out when we are not glued to the real world. Such people overlook their own lifetime production of some eight dreams a night. Dreams are dramatic presentations of the basic issues of an individual's life. It is their difficult language of symbolism that puts off all but the hardy searcher. Suppose you wished to become a dream maker. Here is what you should do. You live in intimate association with a person. Your task is to wait till he sleeps and then present him with an intimate report on the essentials of his life. Your intimacy is so subtle and full of feeling that you know, for instance, that even breakfast cereal has the meaning of a close family gathering. You also know more than the dreamer does. You know that intimate family gatherings are not only pleasant, they are also root and branch of this person's way of spiritual development. But in your wisdom, you wish to speak in a coded message that leaves him free. Both your intimacy and your wish to leave him free would incline you to use a symbolic language of parable, what Swedenborg calls the language of correspondences. But there is another reason for symbolism. It is a very wisely condensed language that can say several things simultaneously. You can deal with all levels from the trivial to the celestial simultaneously in parable. So, as dream maker, you will speak to the person out of the innermost nature of his life in a symbolic, dramatic language of living events in a way that does not impair his freedom.

Let's create one. At this time the individual is losing his way. His spiritual development grows out of regular small intimate gatherings such as those at the breakfast table. He doesn't quite know this. He thinks it is just more pleasant to have everyone together at breakfast. He has temporarily lost this thread of his spiritual development. He is becoming scattered into other concerns. We must remind him. So here is the dream. He falls asleep and we put him through this experience. He is in the kitchen; it is a bit dark (the understanding is poor); people are rushing by (rushing rather that strolling, scattering rather than gathering); a large package of breakfast cereal falls over and scatters (much is involved here). He is trying to gather it in when he is awakened. This condensed message says, where you are, it is dark; people are rushing too much and scattering. You need to gather in. It is presented as breakfast cereal because, to him, what is involved doesn't seem too important when he's awake. "I don't know why I was concerned to gather up mere breakfast cereal." But the feeling inside the dream was quite the opposite. It was urgent to gather up these grains. The feeling inside the dream is always correct. On one level it says your life is scattering and you need to gather in. On a deeper level the way is being pointed towards his spiritual development and grain means interior goods and truths (see Swedenborg's *Arcana Coelestia* 7112). Here is something of a message from the One who lives in intimate association with us, the One concerned about the quality of our life while essentially leaving us in freedom. But this is a process that most dismiss as useless fancy. Breakfast cereal indeed!

The basic process underlying dreams is the same as the language of correspondences that Swedenborg later came to see as a central key to understanding all spiritual matters. In the *Journal of Dreams* we see Swedenborg beginning to experience and grasp this language. In fact, the early part of the *Journal* shows that Swedenborg already has had some experience in these matters. At the outset he was grasping his dreams far better than his contemporaries. Yet his understanding of this language of parable grew more certain as the *Journal* progressed. This is not to say that an individual's personal dream imagery and the correspondences in the Bible are exactly the same, but that they reflect the same process. In the Bible the Lord is speaking to people in terms of the intimate experiences of races of people, whereas in the case above, the speaking is to a man in terms of his personal life experience. The process is the same. In fact, one of the central implications of *The Natural Depth in Man*[2] is that this process, which writes dreams and various other inner processes, is an inherent, natural one. Everyone has it, whether or not he cares a fig for symbolism. There are experiments showing it can't really be shut off. Experimentally cutting off dreaming tends to make dreaming spread into waking consciousness. In fact this is the most fundamental of all processes underlying consciousness. No matter what is done to limit or impair mental functioning, it will only serve to awaken this innermost process. For instance, try to cut out all sensory input, with a person floating blind, deaf and fetal-like in warm water. Does such a person become unconscious without all this sense data to keep him oriented? Not at all. The inner natural symbolic dream maker comes forth in flaming colors.[3] The religious, usually remiss about looking at the depths of human experience, discard dreaming and allied states as of doubtful use. Clinical psychologists make use of it but rarely see its religious implications. Devoted followers of Swedenborg would rather overlook the fact that he studied his dreams at the very time he

---

[2]W. Van Dusen, *The Natural Depth in Man*, Harper and Row, New York, 1972.

[3]The author participated in sensory deprivation experiments and wrote the foreword to C. Brownfield, Isolation, Random House, New York, 1966.

was becoming a seer. It is as though we have compartmented our knowledge and have difficulty seeing that, what is taken as a simple personal experience, also has broader religious implications. If we were concerned only to give our subject above a deeper religious experience, we should have given him the same dream. Yet, it appears, the dream maker is concerned with the whole range of our life experience. The message to our subject above is suitable for eating better, turning from scattering to gathering, bringing peace to him and his family and returning him to his personal, natural spiritual path.

Get the picture of being inside the person's intimate life details and you can begin to interpret dreams. It isn't an intellectual process but rather one of trying to feel with the person. It helps very much to try to visualize being caught in the same dream to get the feeling of what is going on. Let us, then, look at one of the dreams in Swedenborg's *Journal:*

> Stood behind a machine, that was set in motion by a wheel; the spokes entangled me more and more and carried me up so that it was impossible to escape; wakened. (*JD* 18)

Swedenborg was a mining engineer. He had done many careful drawings of such machinery. He was trying to improve mining processes and this involved new and better machines. Let us try to enter the experience to see if we can feel what it is talking about. We are *standing behind* a machine. Normally we'd feel safe and not involved *in* the machine. It must be big. Great big intermeshed wheels. Oh, oh! We are getting involved in it more and more, caught in its spokes. Here we go. It is frightening. We are caught in the spokes and being carried upwards. There is no escape. There is a helpless feeling. We can hear the great wheels grinding, moving, carrying us, inexorably. What will happen? We awaken.

Notice the drama. At first we are standing behind, less involved, not caught up. Then we become involved, caught up. Swedenborg the engineer could stand by, not get caught up. This is one of the earliest dreams in the *Journal.* He was being caught and carried up. Though it may be frightening, the usual implication of up is toward what is higher, the spiritual. If, as dream maker, we wanted to say to Swedenborg, "You engineer! you thought you could stand by and not be involved. Now you are caught up in what is immense and somewhat frightening," we would devise a dream like this.

Swedenborg had an advantage over us: he could feel into the details of his life to read the associations of the dream. We have the advantage over him in that we can look at the nature of his life and see what was to come, what he was being carried towards.

Let us look at his associations to the above dream.

> Signifies either that I ought to be kept more strictly; or perhaps it referred to the lungs of the fetus in the womb, about which I was writing immediately afterwards, or both. (*JD* 18)

What are associations? The dream is made out of inner aspects of the life itself. Associations are the interconnections within this life. When helping someone to work out a dream it makes considerable difference what level within the life is reflected in their associations. The more they are like intellectual constructions from near conscious, the less value they have. The more they represent what is affectively significant to the person, the more central the association. All associations are correct to some extent and are to be respected. But the associations that grip the life are the deeper and more significant. For instance, if the dreamer suddenly feels, with a burst of feeling that such and such means so and so, this association is central and becomes a significant key to the meaning of the dream. It isn't a matter of being biased towards feeling, it is a key to how fully and centrally the life is involved. The most central drift of all these dreams of Swedenborg is from a rather cool, detached intellectual approach to the inner life, to a deeper and deeper emotional involvement.

The above associations say several things. Though they are at the beginning of the dream journal they indicate he already has some experience with inner processes. Wheels and machinery are taken symbolically as having some reference to his life. He is evidently unsure of the meaning. These associations are shallow, not wrong, but near intellect and hence not too deep. "Signifies that I ought to be kept more strictly...." That's pretty good. It captures some of the quality of being caught in the spokes of the wheel. But kept in what way, in his scientific work or in the pursuit of the inner life? The next association to the lungs of a fetus stems from the fact that he was doing work in anatomy at that time. In part this was an interpretation of a symbol with a symbol, something that easily occurs when one is at the beginning of penetrating this process. How can we know "fetal lungs" is a symbol? *Everything of dreams is made from the life of the person and reflects the person.* If fetal lungs represent him, then they too are symbolic. If we went to Swedenborg's later works to see what fetal lungs represent, we would discover that being fetal, they point to the very beginning, and that lungs have to do with understanding. Translation: "I am caught in the very beginning of understanding of a process which is larger than I and carries me up." This fits the context of his whole life and especially the spiritual development which was to occur soon. There is another sign here that Swedenborg was on the right track in understanding this process. He could accept that the dream may have two levels of meaning at once, that he should be "kept strictly," and "fetal lungs." He was ready to abandon the rather linear and limited quality of logical consciousness (especially characteristic of a lifelong scientist) towards the more pervasive spread of meaning in the inner process. Something can have two very different meanings. His grasp of the nature of the process that caught him up grew rapidly during the few months of this *Journal*. He began the *Journal* with a good beginner's sense of the language of the inner life and showed himself to be a fast learner.

Let us try the next dream together to make sure you can enter and begin to understand the process reflected in this *Journal*.

> Was in a garden which had many divisions; pretty; of these I wished to possess one for myself; but looked about to see if there was any way to get out. It appeared to me that I saw one, and thought of another. There was a person who picked away a number of invisible creeping things, and killed them; he said they were bugs, which someone had dropped there and thrown in, and which infected the people there. I did not see them, but saw another creeping thing which I dropped on a white linen cloth beside a woman. It was the uncleanness which ought to be rooted out of me. (*JD* 19)

Enter the experience. See the pretty garden. If you were Swedenborg's dream maker, what is a garden? It is a place where life blossoms verdantly. Swedenborg notices the garden has many divisions. It is ordered, laid out, structured. This is not surprising, for all his life he had been noticing the structure of things. Even his later theology was a garden of many divisions. He wants to possess at least one. Sad, but none of this is *his* yet. This is to say that this verdancy he is walking in, while asleep, seems alien to him. None of it is his. This is another way of expressing this otherness and also his first attitude towards this verdancy in himself. It is similar to standing behind the wheel in the first dream. It is a desire to detach oneself. How shall I get out of here: this way? that? He is a thinker not imbued with the wonder of the garden, even though it is beautiful. What is really going on in this verdancy within? Someone is picking away a number of invisible creeping things. Too bad; the garden is contaminated in a way that can't be seen on the surface. Someone had infested the garden almost carelessly (had dropped and thrown in). This infested the people there, namely Swedenborg himself. What are these bugs? Anything that tends to contaminate and destroy this verdancy of life. Though someone (some force in Swedenborg) is catching and killing off this contamination, the implication is, there is a lot more. What the infestation is, is not yet clear. But finally he sees a creeping thing and drops it on a white cloth beside a woman. A creeping bug, dropped on a white cloth. The scene suggests a contrast of good (white cloth) and evil (a bug). In fact, like good and evil, the bug shows up better in contrast to a white cloth. But why white cloth next to a woman? The image says the purity of the white cloth and the woman are associated. Swedenborg's own association is that the dream says some kind of impurity is to be rooted out of him. This certainly fits with the whole drama and feeling of the dream. It may be he had in mind some particular kind of impurity (he says *the* uncleanness which ought to be rooted out).

Can we know precisely what the bugs in the garden are? It is actually intimated in the dream, but difficult to see. I believe Swedenborg only partly understood it at this point. My guess is that he saw the uncleanness as indicative of lust or pride, or both. The value of a long series of dreams is that any mistakes we make in one dream can gradually be straightened out as the inner process sends its nightly messages in countless different ways. The bugs and women are within a central theme being dealt with in his dreams.

Actually, the impurity has been described in this dream; the reader, however, has the added advantage of knowing Swedenborg's life and this whole dream series quite well. One is in a beautiful garden, it is structured, one wants to own part, and one is thinking how to get away from it. Condensed, one wants to own and control one's relationship to this life. What are bugs in a garden but self-willed bits of life that don't act as one wishes. If they did as the gardener wished, there would be no problem. Gardeners don't mind bees who pollinate. Swedenborg wishes to own, control, but remain aloof from this life. This attitude leaves him contaminated. The bug which is brought into clear focus on the white cloth is specifically a "creeping thing." No fragment of a dream is a useless piece of information. Swedenborg's later revelation was to say creeping things represent the intellectual memory-knowledge of the external man (*Arcana Coelestia* 40). This is the "bug" that spoils the garden of life—the intellectual, rational, external man that would like to own, control, but not be controlled by life (stand behind the machine rather than be caught up). This is the tendency to be rooted out. But, it would be quite sufficient for the reader to get a sense that there is a garden of life in this man but something of him contaminates this life and needs to be rooted out.

Now that you have some sympathy with the process involved and can wander within this murky drama, let us talk of the dramatic sweep of all these dreams. To understand Swedenborg it is necessary to accept that he was really a very intellectual scientist. If you don't have a solid grasp of this, read his several volumes on the senses, genital organs, brain, and chemistry as a starter. Here is a giant intellect attempting to understand everything.

Having exhausted all known areas of human knowledge, he chose to explore within himself in the most direct way possible, by a very close study of inner processes. In the *Journal of Dreams* (222, 261, 267) there are visions, trances, and hypnogogic experiences. Appreciate, too, the time and context of this inner exploration. There were no psycho-analysts, no depth psychologists; the unconscious was yet to be discovered. There was virtually no real understanding at all of these inner processes or dreams except by isolated monks and mystics. It was *terra incognita*, an unknown land that he proposed to risk his life and sanity exploring. He had no one to consult, no books, no help except inwardly. This was unquestionably a daring venture.

There was, however, a kind of guidance in this exploration. His supreme value was to know and experience God. This is a central theme in this *Journal.* He was cheered when he had some kind of experience of the Divine (*JD* 39, 51-4, 127, 167, 276) and downcast when he felt removed from the Divine. He entered dream exploration partly to see what was really there, just as he had all the prior sciences, but mostly to encounter the Divine. Hence we find prayer and visions of the Divine mixed in this process. This was Swedenborg's conscious side of the equation. He was a very intellectual scientist trying to know God by digging deeply into his own life. Anyone who has ventured into this same area will appreciate how hard he tried.

Now let us try to see the development between Swedenborg and the inner process. Until he actually had intimations that the Divine was within and was reaching out a hand to him, he was really uncertain what he was getting into. Even with odd experiences such as the doubling of his thoughts (*JD* 174: he was aware of an idea and its opposite, his intellectual controls being overwhelmed), he did not really fear insanity. He feared that it might not be meaningful, that it might not help him reach the Divine, his real goal. In fact the whole drama was a kind of upwardly inclined spiral. In short periods of time he would feel up and down, but his overall progress towards the Divine was almost inexorably upwards.

In an early dream Swedenborg described himself as impure and unworthy (*JD* 19). This was true, but probably not in the sense he suspected. By far the greatest task the inner had to accomplish was to bring this massive intellect to a *feelingful understanding* of life itself. At several points he thought the dreams were concerned with his scientific work (*JD* 18, 243, 244) in the same way he was. They weren't. The inner process called them a heavy load (*JD* 31). The inner was trying to bring him into a feelingful understanding, an understanding based directly on personal life experience. Among other symbols it spoke of this in terms of his relations with women (feeling). He wanted a woman (to join with this inner realm of life feeling) but he was unworthy. He thought of them sexually, but sex was prohibited. Whatever sexual experience he had had in earlier years, actual sexuality had been put aside for some time according to the dreams. His problem with his own feelings was that he had to consider them in their own nature by entering their realm sympathetically. Yet, this intellect was worried about what he might be getting into. At the shallowest level his unworthiness was that he was lustful and had to put aside sex. That had mostly been done. More seriously, and at a deeper level, his unworthiness was that he was daring to grasp the Divine *on his own terms*, that is intellectually. The inner process simply could not permit this. He had done all these volumes on anatomy before in an effort to find the soul. The soul could be found, represented here as a beautiful woman, but he had to struggle emotionally to find her. Moreover, he had to *become emotional* to find her. In a way the last recorded conscious thoughts at the end of the *Journal* reflect the path he had come over.

> Truths or virgins of this sort think it base to be exposed to sale; they regard themselves as so precious and dear to their admirers that they think it an indignity if anyone bids for them; still more so if he comes to buy them. Others, who regard them as of no account, they treat superciliously. So then, in order that they may not fall under valuation by the former, nor into contempt from the latter, they prefer to offer themselves gratui-

tously to their lovers. I, who am their servant, do
not dare to disobey them, for fear of being deprived
of their service. (*JD* 286)

What did he seek? Truth. But truth has been trans-
formed. She is like a lovely virgin and the way she
feels must be understood. No one can buy her.
Those who think little of her, she treats superciliously. She prefers to give herself to one who *loves*
her.

The central change that takes place in the *Journal of Dreams* is that the very basis of his understanding was shifted by this inward exploration. His
understanding had become affectional, thereby
becoming living. Formerly there was unworthiness.
He had tried to buy truth, paying a price of intellectual analysis. He too, had undervalued her when he
doubted and undervalued this inner process. Now
he had found the way. The real truth, what hadn't
been known before (a virgin) was given freely to a
lover, for the lover had come sympathetically into
her real nature.

The *Journal of Dreams* has been relatively ne-
glected by Swedenborg scholars because they didn't
fully sense what was involved. There was some
scandalous talk when this was first published in its
original Swedish because of the few sexual references. The one complete English edition had all the
sexual passages in Latin. The scandal was foolish.
These people hadn't looked at their own far more

sexual dreams. Compared to an average series of dreams, sex is probably under-represented here. One psychoanalyst concluded Swedenborg was homosexual. He hadn't seen the obvious heterosexuality of these dreams. Some have said[4] that Swedenborg had a sexual problem. It has to be seen in context. It was the effort to control natural desire in an unmarried man which made it seem like a problem. Sexual desire disappeared during the writing of the *Journal.* The intimate association of the dream maker leads it to use rude symbols. The rudest example here is the *vagina dentata,* a vagina with teeth (*JD* 120, 261). Modern dream analysts have found the same symbol. This was one of the several ways in which Swedenborg's difficulty (teeth) with feeling (vagina) was expressed. In a way the flap over sex in these dreams is appropriate, for the relationship to women (his own feeling side) was a central issue of the dreams. It was as though this great explorer wanted to know God on his own terms (intellectual, rational and in control) and learned that he would have to experience his own feeling side in order to enter into the love of God. He could not know God except by becoming more like Him. This is also the model of the relationship between personal and spiritual development.

---

[4]See e.g. Colin Wilson's introduction to the Dole translation of *Heaven and Hell,* Swedenborg Foundation, New York, 1976.

There are two precognitive dreams in this series (*JD* 243, 250). Until one wrestles with dreams and comes to appreciate their wisdom, it is difficult to believe that the dream maker also sees one's future. There is good evidence for this.[5] The difficulty is that, in the midst of a welter of symbolism, the dreamer usually has trouble seeing what is talking of the future and what is simply portraying the present. In one, the dream (250) referred to Swedenborg's book, *The Worship and Love of God*. But Swedenborg hadn't even thought of writing it yet, let alone figure out its title. He thought the dream referred to his rather dry, intellectual work on the infinite. The whole dream (249-252) is worth looking at, for it deals directly with the central problem of bringing him away from intellect into love. The dream casually speaks of a book he had not yet conceived, a book that was to be a bursting forth of passionate understanding. The other dream is of even more interest for it very informally says Swedenborg is to be admitted into heaven and hell, as later happened.

> I saw a gable of the most beautiful palace that could possibly be seen; glory like the sun upon it. It was said to me that in the society it was decided

---

[5]Jan Ehrenwald, *New Dimensions of Deep Analysis*, Allen and Unwin, New York, 1954.

that I should be a member that was immortal,
which no one previously had been except one who
had been dead and had lived again. Others said
that there were several. (*JD* 243)

Here his future entry into heaven and hell is casually described. He used the gable end of a palace
more than once as though it meant an ideal place.
Apparently it had been decided that he was to be
one of the few mortals to explore heaven and hell.
Curiously, he thought perhaps he was the only one
to have this experience, while "others said there
were several."

One final scene from beyond this journal will
round out the drama here. Swedenborg's friend Robsahm[6] recollected asking Swedenborg whether any
other person could come into the same degree of
spirituality in which he was. Swedenborg warned
him that this could lead to insanity if a person
"from his natural man and by his own speculations
tries to fathom heavenly things which transcend his
comprehension." Here was the central uncleanliness
that was to be eliminated in this dream series. He
goes on to describe the day when he was admitted
into heaven and hell. He was in London at an inn.
He had eaten heartily and engaged in much discus-

---

[6] R. L. Tafel, *Documents Concerning Swedenborg*, 2 vols.,
Swedenborg Society, London, 1875-1877. Vol I, p. 34.

sion. Then he unaccountably entered a vision. The room grew dark (darkness of understanding) and the floor was covered with crawling reptiles, snakes, frogs and similar creatures. Then the darkness suddenly cleared and there was a man in the room with him. "I was very much frightened at his words, for he said 'Eat not so much.'" In terror he hastened home. Again, the man appeared and revealed he was the Lord God and that Swedenborg was to be guided in what he was to write. That same night, according to Robsahm, he was fully introduced into heaven and hell, an experience that was to remain his whenever he wanted for many years. Dream 243 becomes real. But why "Eat not so much"? I believe with the scholar Alfred Acton that the reference was to excess on his part in presuming to know so much in philosophical discussion, for his mission was to be guided by the Lord. He "swallows too much," who presumes of his own powers. Creeping things represent the dangers of presumptuous speculation. With this final warning of the uncleanliness to be removed, he became a servant of the Lord. His writings thereafter are in marked contrast to the earlier ones. Where he endlessly speculated before, there is not a trace of speculation in his theology. There he describes what he has been given to know, what he has seen and experienced. His later writings are full of feeling and show much concern with love and affection.

There are several important lessons in this volume. The Divine is within and can be known, but the process is one of struggle and search. It is just as well that the very language of dreams requires us to enter into the somewhat alien and intimate ways of the inner process. We must stretch and change to understand it. The process of spiritual development requires personal growth. The person who would try to reach the Divine by his conventional viewpoint of consciousness finds he must change, expand, become anew in unexpected directions before the Divine can be known. If we can really learn to read this account, to get "caught in the spokes of the wheel" as he was, then we can also begin to read the patiently sent messages we receive every night. In Swedenborg's uncertainty, doubt, and struggle, we should see something of ourselves and take heart. For we all are like Emanuel Swedenborg, by the grace of God, caught in the spokes of a great wheel.

SWEDENBORG'S JOURNAL OF DREAMS

[1][1] 1743, the 21st of July, I travelled from Stock-holm, arrived on the 27th at Ystad, after passing through Tälje, Nyköping, Norrköping, Linköping, Grenna, and Jonköping. In Ystad I met the Countess de la Gardie,[2] with her two daughters, and the two counts, Count Fersen,[3] Major Landtishusen[4] and Magister Klingenberg. On the 31st General Stenflycht[5] arrived with his son, and Capt. Schachta.[6]

---

[1] The paragraph numbering is that adopted by C. Th. Odhner in his 1918 English translation.

[2] The Countess De la Gardie was the widow of Count Magnus Julius De la Gardie, who died in 1743. See *Spiritual Diary* n. 6027.

[3] Count Frederik Axel von Fersen (1719-1794) was an eminent aristocrat and politician who married the daughter of Countess De la Gardie in 1752.

[4] Jakob Albrekt von Lantingshausen (1699-1769) was an eminent Swedish soldier and politician. In 1743 he went to Paris to enter the French army and take part in the War of Austrian Secession. In 1748 he married a sister of Count F. A. von Fersen.

[5] Johan Stenflycht (1681-1758) was a Swedish soldier who distinguished himself in the 1713 battle of Gadebusch. In 1743 he was commander-in-chief at Hamburg.

[6] Captain Schachta, probably the same as the "Kapten Schiechta" mentioned by Linnaeus in his *Anteckningar*. (See Tafel *Doc.* II, p. 1068.)

[2] The wind was against us, and we did not sail till the 5th of August; I was in company with General Stenflycht. On the 6th we reached Stralsund, and early on the 7th entered the town. The countess and the general continued their journey the same day.

[3] In Stralsund I again visited the fortress from Badenthore, to Francken, Stripseer and Kniperthore, and the house where King Charles XII lodged, the Mejerfeldz palace; the churches of St. Nicholas; of St. James, which was laid in ruins during the siege; and of St. Mary. I paid a visit to Colonel and Commandant Swerjn,[7] Superintendent Löper, and Post-director Crivits. In St. Nicholas Church a timepiece is shown which was struck by lightning in 1670, 1683, and 1688, just as the hand pointed to 6:00. I afterwards visited some new fortifications outside Kniperthore. I met Carl Jesper Benzelius.[8] Visited the waterworks that supply the town: they consist of two sets of pipes.

[4] The 9th of August, travelled from Stralsund through Damgarten: through the Mecklenburg

---

[7]Count Claus Philip von Schwerin (1689-1748).

[8]Carl Jesper Benzelius (1714-1793) was the second son of Eric Benzelius and Swedenborg's sister Anna. In 1743 he was on a journey to Germany. In 1766 he became Bishop of Strengnäs. He was very friendly to Swedenborg and corresponded with some of his early followers in Sweden.

territory past Rimnits, to Röstock, where I visited eight churches, five large and three small, a cloister for ladies, eight in number, who however are not under rules of restraint.

[5] From there I journeyed to Wismar, where there are six churches, the best are those of St. Mary and St. George.

Thence on the 11th; and on the way visited Gadebuch, the scene of the battle between the Swedes and Danes; afterwards to Ratzeburg; which is surrounded by swamp, over which a long bridge leads into the town.

[6] On the 12th came to Hamburg, and took up my quarters in the Keisershof. The Countess de la Gardie was staying in the same hotel. Met Baron Hamilton,[9] Reuterholm,[10] Trivalt,[11] König,[12] Assessor

---

[9]Baron Carl Fredrik Hamilton in 1743 attended crown-prince elect Adolph Frederik as marshal of the court. (See Tafel *Doc.* II, p. 1065.)

[10]Baron Esbjorn Kristian Reuterholm (1710-1773) was a Swedish politician, royal chamberlain, and senator.

[11]Samuel Triewald (1688-1743) was a Swedish scientist and writer.

[12]Johan Fredrik König in 1738 became the Swedish agent and in 1747 resident consul of the Swedish Postal Commissary in Hamburg. He died in 1759. (See Tafel *Doc.* II, p. 82.)

Awerman: was presented to Prince Augustus,[13] his royal highness' brother, who talked Swedish: afterwards was presented by the Grand Marshal Lesch to his Royal Highness Adolph Fredrich;[14] delivered the manuscripts I had with me, and which are for the press, and at the same time showed the reviews of the former works.

[7] The 17th, travelled from Hamburg, over the river to Buxtehude, where, for the space of a mile I saw the prettiest country I had seen in Germany; the route lay through a continuous garden of apples, pears, plums, walnuts, chestnut trees, limes and elms.

[8] The 18th, to Bremen, with its fine ramparts and suburbs; the best of these is Nystadt; by the bridge leading thither, there are no less than eleven water mills, one by the side of the other. Visited the town house in the market place, and also the great Rolan [belfry], which is the sign of a free town: afterwards went to St. Nicholas and the cathedral

---

[13]Prince Augustus of Holstein-Gottorp was a younger brother of Adolph Frederik.

[14]Adolph Frederik, Duke of Holstein-Gottorp, was elected crown prince of Sweden on July 3, 1743, three weeks before Swedenborg met him. He succeeded to the throne in 1751. The "manuscripts [delivered"] were of the *Animal Kingdom*, which he was about to publish at The Hague. The "reviews" were of the *Economy of the Animal Kingdom*.

churches; was also in the hospital where there are several statues.

[9] 20th, from Bremen to Leer, through Oldenburg, which is a country belonging to the King of Denmark; fine fortifications, with plenty of water about them: went also through Neuskants: at Leer there is a fort which is called Leerort, which is in the possession of Holland. Thence to Gröningen, which is a large town, under the Prince of Orange. At Leewarden I saw his palace, as well as his mother's; the latter is called the Princess' Palace; visited also the hotel de ville, and other places. I came here by *Treckscheut* [passenger boats on the Dutch canals drawn by horses. *Translator*].

[10] From Gröningen there is a choice of two routes, namely, to Harlingen, and to Lemmer; to the former, the mode of conveyance is by *Treckscheut*; to the latter, by coach. I chose the way to Harlingen through Leewarden.

From Harlingen, which is a large town...[the continuation is missing.[15] It is impossible to decide whether it was ever written, or not, for the word *stad* (town) concludes the sixth page, and then come several blank leaves; yet it is probable that some leaves (4?) have been torn out. On the shreds that remain of two that have been cut out, there are

---

[15]Any remaining entries in the manuscript could not have been lengthy, as all that was left to tell was of the short journey from Harlingen to The Hague.

large numeral figures written in an unpracticed hand, perhaps a child's. *Editor.*]

[11] 1. Dreamed of my youth and the Gustavian family.[16]

2. In Venice,[17] of the beautiful palace.

3. In Sweden, of the white expanse of heaven.

4. In Leipsic, of one that lay in boiling water.

5. Of one that tumbled with a chain down into the deep.

6. Of the king that gave away so precious a thing in a peasant's cabin.

7. Of the man servant that wished me to go away on my travels.

[12] 8. Of my delights during the nights. Wondered at myself for having nothing left to do for my own honor, so that I was even touched. Also at not being at all inclined towards the sex, as I had previously been all my life.

9. How I was in waking trances nearly the whole time.

[13] 10. How I set myself against the spirit.

---

[16]The "Gustavian family" was the royal dynasty of Sweden, founded by Gustavus Wasa. The last remaining members in Swedenborg's youth were Charles XII and Ulrica Eleonora.

[17]Swedenborg sojourned in Venice from April to August, 1738.

And how I then favored it, but found afterwards that it was madness, devoid of all life and connection.

And that thus a quantity of what I have written must be of the same kind; because I had not at all resisted the power of the spirit to that degree; inasmuch as the faults are all my own, but the truths are not mine.

Indeed I sometimes fell into impatience and into thoughts [doubts], and would fain have given way to insolent demand whenever the matter did not go so easily as I wished, as I did nothing for my own sake: but I was a long way from finding out my own unworthiness, or being grateful for mercies.

[14] 11. How I found, after I arrived at The Hague, that my interest, and self love in my work, had passed away; at which I myself wondered.

How the inclination to the other sex so suddenly ceased which had been my strongest passion.

How I had, during the whole time, the best sleep at nights, which was more than kind.

How my trances were, before and after sleep. My clear thoughts about things.

[15] How I set myself against the power of the Holy Spirit, what happened thereupon; how I saw hideous specters, without life horribly shrouded and moving in their shrouds; together with a beast that attacked me, but not the child.

[16] It seemed I lay on a mountain with a gulf under it: there were knolls upon it; I lay there and

tried to help myself up, holding by a knoll, without foothold; a gulf was below. It signifies, that I myself wish to help myself from the abyss of hell, which is not possible to be done.

[17] How a woman laid down by my side, just as if I was waking. I wished to know who it was. She spoke slowly; said that she was pure, but that I smelled ill. It was my guardian angel, as I believe, for then began the temptation.

1744. March 24-25.

[18] 1. Stood behind a machine, that was set in motion by a wheel; the spokes entangled me more and more and carried me up so that it was impossible to escape; wakened. Signifies either that I ought to be kept more strictly; or perhaps it referred to the lungs of the fetus in the womb,[18] about which I was writing immediately afterwards, [or] both.

[19] 2. Was in a garden which had many divisions; pretty; of these I wished to possess one for myself; but looked about to see if there was any way to get out. It appeared to me that I saw one, and thought of another. There was a person who picked away a number of invisible creeping things, and killed them; he said they were bugs, which someone had dropped there and thrown in, and which

---

[18]This subject is referred to in the *Animal Kingdom*, Vol. 1, n. 272.

infested the people there. I did not see them, but
saw another little creeping thing which I dropped on
a white linen cloth beside a woman. It was the
uncleanness which ought to be rooted out from me.

[20] 3. Descended a great staircase, which ended
in a ladder; freely and boldly; below there was a
hole, which led down into a great abyss. It was
difficult to reach the other side without falling into
the hole. There were on the other side persons to
whom I reached my hand, to help me over, wakened. Signifies the danger I am in of falling into hell,
if I do not get help.

[21] 4. Spoke with our successor[19] in Sweden
(who was turned into a woman) freely and familiarly;
afterwards with Carl Broman,[20] bidding him beware
of him; he answered something.

Spoke with Erland Broman,[21] and told him I was

---

[19]"Our successor" refers to Adolph Frederik.

[20]Carl Broman (1703-1784) was Master of Ceremonies at the
Swedish court, governor of Elfsborg (1749), governor of Stockholm (1751). Swedenborg had invested 10,000 dalers of his
capital with him.

[21]Erland Broman (1704-1757), a younger brother of Carl
Broman, became court marshal in 1741 and president of the
College of Commerce in 1747. He was a favorite of King Frederik
I, acting as intermediary in the king's love intrigues. He married
Countess Wilhelmina Taube, a sister of the king's chief mistress.
Swedenborg identified him with "luxury, riches and pride," and
in the *Spiritual Diary*, n. 5492-5495, describes his death-bed
                                                    (continued...)

here again. Do not at all know what it means, unless something of the following.

[22] 5. Came into a magnificent room and spoke with a lady who was a court attendant; she wished to tell me something; then the queen entered, and went through into another apartment. It seemed to me it was the same that had represented our successor. I went out, for I was very meanly dressed, having just come off a journey; a long old overcoat without hat or wig. I wondered that she deigned to come after me. She said that a person[22] had given to his mistress all the jewels; but he got them back in this manner; it was told to her that he had not given the best; then she threw the jewels away.

[23] She asked me to come in again; but I excused myself on the ground of being so shabbily dressed, and having no wig: I must first go home. She said it was of no consequence. It means that I

---

[21](...continued)
repentance as being of no avail.

[22]This was probably Frederik I (1676-1751), landgrave of Hesse Cassel who married Ulrica Eleonora in 1714, through whose influence he ascended to the Swedish throne in 1720. The "mistress" referred to was probably Hedwig Ulrica Taube.

should then write and begin the epilogue[23] to the second part, to which I wished to put a prologue, but it is not needed. I did accordingly. What she related about the jewels means truths, which are revealed to a man, but are withdrawn again; for she was angry because she did not get all. I afterwards saw the jewels in hands, and a great ruby in the middle of them.

[March] 25-26.

[24] It seemed I took a key, went in, was examined by the door keeper as to what keys I had; showed them all; also as to whether I should have two. But it seemed that Hesselius[24] had another. I was taken into custody, and watched. Many people came to me in vehicles. It seemed to me that I had done nothing wrong. Yet it came to mind that it might look suspicious if it was asked how it happened that I had taken the key. Wakened. Many significations: as, that I had taken the key to anatomy: the other, that Hesselius had, was the key to

---

[23]This epilogue is found at the end of Vol. 1 of *Regnum Animale.*

[24]Dr. Johan Hesselius (1687-1752), an eminent physician and botanist, was Swedenborg's cousin. He accompanied Swedenborg on a journey to Holland in 1721.

medicine. Also that the key to the lungs[25] is the pulmonary artery, which is thus the key to all the motion of the body, or it may be interpreted spiritually.

[25] I entreated a cure for my sickness; a lot of rags were given me to buy; I took the half of them, and selected from the other half; but gave the rags all back again. He said that he himself would buy me something that would serve for a cure. It was my body's thoughts that were the rags wherewith I would cure myself; but it was no good.

[26] Came out afterwards, and saw many black images; a black one was thrown to me: I saw that it could not fit to the foot. It meant that natural reason could never harmonize with spiritual, I believe.

[March] 30-31.

[27] Saw a number of women; one who was writing a letter. Took it; but do not know where it went. She was sitting, and a yellow man smote her upon the back; he wished that she should have more stripes; but this was enough. It concerns, so I believe, what I am writing, and have written; our philosophy.

---

[25]Swedenborg was then preparing for the press the second part of *Regnum Animale*, which treats of the lungs and connecting organs.

[28] Saw also a very lovely woman as it were beside a window there, where a child was placing roses. She took me by the hand and led me. It betokens what I am writing; also my torment, that would lead me; so I believe.

[29] Saw a procession of men; magnificent; jewelled; so fine that I never saw anything finer; but it disappeared soon. It was, as I believe, experience, which now is in great luxuriance.[26]

April 1-2.

[30] Rode in the air on horseback. Went into all the rooms, kitchen, and the rest, and sought after a particular person; but found nothing. The rooms were badly swept and cared for. At last, I was carried in the air into a hall; there I got two pieces of beautiful bread, and so I again got him [whom I sought]. Here there were a number of people, and a well-swept room. Signifies the Lord's Supper.

[31] King Charles[27] sat in a dark room, and spoke something, but very indistinctly; afterwards asked a person at the table if he had not heard what he had asked. He said, "Yes." Afterwards he shut the

---

[26]Odhner's translation reads: "It was, as I believe, experimental science which now is greatly in fashion."

[27]Charles XII, King of Sweden 1697-1718, with whom Swedenborg was closely associated from 1715 to 1718.

window, and I helped him with the curtains. After this I got up on a horse, but by no means took the way I thought, but rode over hills and mountains; rode fast; a heavy load followed on to me; I could not succeed in riding away, the horse got tired with the load, and I would have him put in to some one. He came in, and the horse became like a slaughtered and blood-red beast, and lay there. Betokens that I have got all that I had thought for my instruction; and that I am taking a way which is perhaps not the right one. The load was my remaining works that followed me, that on the way became of that kind, weary and dead.

[32] Stepped out of a coach; the coach was driven into a lake; as he was driving it in, the coachman called out to the other coach to take care: there was also danger when he drove in. I looked at the other coach. There seemed to be a screen at the back of it, which was spread out as a screen is [like a fan]. I, in concert with a man that sat at the back, took the screen, went in, and bound it together. Meaning was, that the beginning of my work was difficult; the second coach was warned and bid to take care: presages also that I ought to draw the sails together, to furl them; and not make the notes so long.[28]

---

[28]A reference to his work then in progress, *Regnum Animale*, a work with many lengthy footnotes.

[April] 2-3.

[33] There came two persons. They came into a house which was not yet ready, but the building finished. They went round about it, and did not appear at all pleased with it. We saw that our force was not with us, and feared them. One came to me, and said that they had a punishment for me on the next Maundy Thursday, if I did not take myself off. I did not know how to get out. He said he would show me the way. Wakened. Means that I, in an unprepared and unswept cabin had invited a visit from the Highest; and that he found it unswept; ought to be punished; but most graciously the way was shown me to escape their wrath.

[34] [It seemed there] was a beggar, that cried out that he would have bacon; they wished to give him something else, but he continually cried out, "Bacon!" Wakened. Same signification, I believe.

[35] Saw two batches of soldiers, blue; they marched in two bodies past my window, which stood ajar. I wished to look out on the first body that marched, which appeared to me to be magnificent. Wakened. It is a gracious guard, to prevent me from perishing.

N.B. April 3-4, 1744
which was the day before Easter.

[36] Found nothing during the whole night,
though I often wakened. Believed all was away, and
settled, and that I was left, or driven off. About the
morning it seemed that I rode, and it was shown me
where to go; but when I looked, it was dark. Found
that in the darkness I had gone astray; but then the
light came, and I saw that I was astray. Saw the
way, and the forests and groves to which I ought to
go, and behind them the sky. Wakened. Then came
the thought of itself about the first life and, in
consequence, about the other life; and it seemed to
me that all is full of grace. Began weeping because
I had not loved at all but instead had continually
angered him that had led me and had shown me
the way that leads at last to the kingdom of grace;
and because I had grown unworthy to be taken to
grace.

[April] 4-5. Went to God's table.

[37] It was told me that a courier was now come.
I said that it might be, that [all the rest is crossed
out with the pen].

A tune was sung, and a line I remember of the hymn:[29]

> Jesus is my best of friends
> *Jesus är min wän then bäste*

It seemed to me that the buds had burst, and were green.

[April] 5-6.

[38] Easter day was the 5th of April. On that day I went to God's table. The temptation still continued, principally after dinner till 6 o'clock, but nothing definite. It was a wretchedness as of final condemnation, and as of being in hell. Still there was always the hope that the Holy Spirit gave; and strength therein, as in Paul, Romans 5:5. The evil one had power given him to make the innermost uneasy with various thoughts.

[39] At Whitsuntide[30] after the Lord's supper, I was exceedingly happy, and yet outwardly afflicted. The temptation came in the afternoon, in quite a different way; but strong; for I was assured of having

---

[29]This refers to a hymn Swedenborg learned in his childhood. It was No. 245 in the original edition of his father's hymn book.

[30]Odhner, following Tafel (see *Doc.* 209, Vol 2, p. 155), corrected this to read "Easter."

got my sins forgiven, and yet I could by no means restrain my flying thoughts from venting a little, against my better judgment; which was the work of the evil one, through permission. Prayer, and also God's Word calmed down these thoughts. Faith was there in full, but trust and confidence and love seemed to be missing.

[40] I went to bed at 9:00 o'clock. The temptation accompanied with trembling continued till 10:30. I then fell into a sleep in which the whole of my temptation was represented to me: how Erland Broman had sought me in different ways, and endeavored to get me to take his side and to belong to that party (luxury, riches, vanity); but he could not manage to win me over. I grew more and more resolutely opposed, because he treated me with contempt. [41] Afterwards I was in strife with a serpent, dark, grey, which lay down, and was Broman's dog. I struck at it with a club many times, but could never hit it on the head; it was in vain. It tried to bite me, but could not. I laid hold of it by its open jaws: it could not bite me; nor could I do it much harm. At last I got it by the jowl and squeezed it hard; also the nose, which I squeezed until poison squirted out. I said that though the dog was not mine, yet as he had wished to bite me, I must correct him. Thereupon he seemed to say that he could not get me to say a word to him; I quarreled then with him. When I wakened, the words I was saying were: "Hold your tongue."

[42] From this it is easy to see without further explanation how the temptation was; and how great God's grace was on the other side, through the merits of Christ and the working of the Holy Spirit; to whom be honor and glory from eternity to eternity. The thought struck me instantly, how great the Lord's grace is, which accounts it to us as if we had stood against temptation, and attributes it to us as our own; when yet it is only God's grace and working; is his and nowise ours and he overlooks all our weakness in the combat, manifold as it has surely been. And moreover what great glory our Lord gives after a little time of adversity.

[43] Afterwards I slept, and it seemed to me that the whole night in various ways I was first brought into association with others, through the sinfulness that existed. Afterwards, that I was bandaged and wrapped in wonderful and indescribable courses of circles; showing that during the whole night I was inaugurated in a wonderful manner. And then it was said "Can any Jacobite be more than honest?" So at last I was received with an embrace. Afterwards it was said that he ought by no means to be called so, or in the way just named; but in some way which I have no recollection of, if it were not Jacobite. This I can by no means explain: it was a mystical series.

[44] Afterwards I wakened and slept again many times, and all was in answer to my thoughts, yet in such wise that there was such a life and such a glory in all that I can give no account of it in the

least; for it was all heavenly; clear for me at the time; but afterwards I can explain nothing of it. In a word, I was in heaven and heard speech that no human tongue with the life in it can utter; nor the glory and innermost delight in the train of the speech.

Except this I was in a waking state, as in a heavenly ecstasy, which also is indescribable.

[45] At 9:00 o'clock I lay down in bed, and got up between 9:00 and 10:00 in the morning, having been in bed between twelve and thirteen hours. To the Highest be thanksgiving, honor, praise! Hallowed be his name: Holy, holy, Lord God of Sabaoth!

[46] How I learned by actual proof the meaning of the injunction not to love the angels better than God; a proof which had nearly spoiled the whole work. But in regard to our Lord, no account ought to be taken of any angel; but in regard to their help, where love is concerned, it is a far lower case.

[47] I found in myself like beams of light that it was the greatest happiness to be a martyr in regard to the indescribable grace connected with love to God, which causes the subject of it to wish to endure this torment, which is nothing in comparison with the everlasting; and makes it the least of things to offer up one's life.

[48] Had also in my mind and my body a kind of consciousness of an indescribable bliss, so that if it had been in a higher degree, the body would have been as it were dissolved in mere bliss. This was the

night between Easter Sunday and Easter Monday; also the whole of Easter Monday.

April 6-7. N.B. N.B. N.B.

[49] In the evening I came into another sort of temptation, namely, between eight and nine o'clock in the evening when I read God's miracles performed through Moses, it seemed to me that somewhat of my understanding mixed itself therein; so that I could never have the strong faith that I ought to have. I believed and did not believe; thought that therefore the angels and God showed themselves to shepherds, but never to the philosopher that lets his understanding take part in the matter. The understanding, for instance, is always bent to ask why he used the wind when he called the locusts together? why he hardened Pharaoh's heart? why he did not do all at once? with more of the like. In my mind I did indeed smile at this, but yet did it so much, that faith was by no means steady. [50] I looked at the fire, and said to myself: Thus I ought also not to believe that the fire exists, and [ought to believe] that the outward senses are more fallacious than what God himself says, which is very truth; I ought rather to believe this than myself. In thoughts like those and many more I passed the first hour or hour and a half, and in my mind smiled at the tempter. It is to be noted, that the same day I went to Delft, and the whole day had the grace to be in

deep spiritual thoughts, so deep and lovely as I had never been in before and this, the whole day; which was the work of the spirit which I then found with me.

[51] At ten o'clock I went to bed and was somewhat better. Half an hour after I heard a noise under my head. I thought that the tempter was then going away. Straightway there came over me a shuddering, so strong from the head downwards and over the whole body, with a noise of thunder, and this happened several times. I found that something holy was upon me; [52] I then fell into a sleep, and at about 12:00, 1:00 or 2:00 in the night, there came over me a strong shuddering from head to foot, with a thundering noise as if many winds beat together; which shook me; it was indescribable and prostrated me on my face. Then, at the time I was prostrated, at that very moment I was wide awake, and saw that I was cast down. [53] Wondered what it meant. And I spoke as if I were awake; but found nevertheless that the words were put into my mouth. "And oh! Almighty Jesus Christ, that thou, of thy so great mercy, deignest to come to so great a sinner. Make me worthy of thy grace." I held together my hands, and prayed, and then came forth a hand, which squeezed my hands hard. [54] Straightway thereupon I continued my prayer, and said, "Thou hast promised to take to grace all sinners; thou canst nothing else than keep thy word." At that same moment, I sat in his bosom,

and saw him face to face; it was a face of holy mien, and in all it was indescribable, and he smiled so that I believe that his face had indeed been like this when he lived on earth. He spoke to me and asked if I had a clear bill of health. I answered, "Lord, thou knowest better than I." "Well, do so," said he; that is, as I found it in my mind to signify; love me in reality; or do what thou hast promised. God give me grace thereto; I found that it was not in my power. Wakened, with shudderings. **[55]** Fell again into such a state that I was in thoughts neither sleeping, nor waking. Thought, What can this be? Is it Christ, God's son, I have seen? But it is sin that I doubt thereof. But as it is commanded that we shall prove the spirits, so I thought it all over and found from what had passed on the previous night that I was purified and enwrapped and protected through the whole night by the Holy Spirit, and in this way prepared hereto; as also that I fell on my face, and the words I spoke; and the prayer, that came by no means from myself, but the word was placed in my mouth; still, that it was I that spoke, and that all was holy. So I found that it was God's own son, who came down with this thunder, and prostrated me to the ground, from himself, and made the prayer, and so, said I, it was Jesus himself. **[56]** I asked for grace, for having so long doubted of this, and also for having let it come into my thoughts to ask for a miracle, which I found was unbecoming. Thereupon I fell to prayer and asked only for grace. More than this I did not utter, yet afterwards I entreated and prayed to have love, which is Jesus Christ's work, and none of mine. Meantime, shudderings often went over me.

[57] Afterwards about daybreak I fell again into a sleep, and then it was chiefly in my thoughts how Christ unites himself to mankind. Holy thoughts came; but they were such that they are quite unsearchable. I cannot in the least convey to the pen what passed; for I only know that I was in such thoughts.

[58] Afterwards I saw my father, in a different costume from that he used to wear, nearly of a red color; he called me to him, and took me by the arms, where I had half sleeves with cuffs or ruffles in front. He pulled both the ruffles forwards, and tied them with my strings. My having ruffles signifies that I am not of the priestly order, but am, and ought to be, a civil servant. Afterwards he asked me how I like the question, that a king has given leave to about 30 persons who were in holy orders to marry, and thus change their estate. I answered that I had thought and written something about such a matter, but it has no relation thereto. **[59]** Instantly thereupon I found [it in me] to answer, according to my conscience, that no one whatsoever should be permitted to alter the estate to which he has devoted himself. He said that he was of the same opinion. But I said, if the king has resolved, the thing is settled. He said he should deliver his vote in writing. If there are 50 [votes] the matter will be settled accordingly. I observed it as a remarkable fact that I never called him my father, but my brother; thought afterwards how this was: it seemed to me that my father was dead, and this, that is my father, must thus be my brother.

[60] To forget nothing, it came also into the thoughts, that the Holy Spirit would show me to Jesus, and present me to him, as a work that he had so prepared: and that I ought by no means to attribute anything to myself; but that all is his; although he of grace, imputes to us the same.

So I sang the hymn I then selected:
Jesus är min wän then bäste, n. 245
[Jesus is my best of friends.]

[61] I have now learned this in spiritual [things], that there is nothing for it but to humble oneself and to desire nothing else, and this with all humility, than the grace of Christ. I attempted of my own to get love, but this is arrogant; for when one has God's grace, one leaves oneself to Christ's good pleasure, and does according to his good pleasure. One is happiest when one is in God's grace. I was obliged with humblest prayers to beg for forgiveness before my conscience could be pacified: for I was still in temptation until this was done. The Holy Spirit taught me this; but I, with my foolish under-

standing, left out humility, which is the foundation of all.

The night between [April] 7th and 8th.

[62] Throughout the whole night I was going down deep, stairs after stairs, and through various places, but quite safely and securely, as if there were no danger in the depth; and then there came to me in the dream this verse: that neither the deep, nor anything else any more...[31]

[63] Afterwards it seemed I was with a number of others dining with a priest. I paid about a louis d'or for my dinner; more in fact than I ought. But as I was on the way therefrom, I had with me two silver cups I had taken away from the table. This pained me, and I endeavored to send them back, and it seemed that I had the means of doing so. This means, I believe, that I, in the temptation, had paid my part (it was God's grace) and even more than I ought (God's grace); but that thereby I learned much about spiritual things; which is meant by the silver cups which I wished to send back to the priest; that is to say, to the glory of God I would again give to the church universal in some manner; as it seems to me indeed may be the case.

---

[31]This is a reference to lines from the third verse of the hymn referred to in note 29, above.

[64] Afterwards I went in a considerable company to a second priest, where it seemed I had been before. When we alighted, it seemed there were so many of us that we should incommode the priest. Thought nothing of our being so many, and of the priest being troubled. This signified that I had many unruly thoughts where I ought not to have them; thoughts that I could never control. The people also that I had before seen resembled Poles, hussars, that are marauders. But it seemed that they went away.

[65] I was also in this temptation, that thoughts invaded me which I should never be able to control; yea, so hard that I was withheld from all other thought; only to give them free rein for once, to go against the power of the spirit, which leads in another direction; so hard, that if God's grace had not been the stronger, I should surely have fallen therein, or gone mad. Meantime I could by no means get my thoughts to contemplate the Christ that I had seen for that short moment. The movement and the power of the spirit came to me, and I felt that I would rather go mad. Hereby was signified my relation to the second priest. **[66]** I can compare it to two scales of a balance, in the one of which is our own will and vehement nature; in the other, God's power, which our Lord so places in temptation that he sometimes lets it come to an equilibrium, but so soon as ever it will weigh down one side, he helps it up. So I have found it, to speak after a natural manner. From this it follows that our power that presses down that scale is little, and that it rather opposes than assists the power of the spirit; and thus it is only our Lord's work, which he disposes.

[67] Then I found that various matters in my thoughts were brought forward that had been put into them long before; and so I found by this example the truth of God's Word, that there is not the smallest word or thought that God does not know; and if we do not obtain God's grace, we are answerable therefore.

[68] This have I learned, that the one only thing in this state (I know not of any other) is, with humility to thank God for his grace, and to pray for it; and for us to regard our own unworthiness and God's infinite grace.

[69] It was wonderful that I could have two thoughts, quite separate, at one and the same time; one for myself, who was occupied entirely by other thoughts, and withal the thoughts of the temptation, in such wise that nothing was available to drive it away; it held me so captive that I did not know whither to fly, for I bore it with me.

[70] Moreover after this again, when particular matters I had long before thought and rooted in my mind came up before me, it was as if it was said to me that I should find reasons to excuse myself; which also was a great temptation; or to attribute to myself the good I had done, or more properly, that

had happened through me. But God's spirit prevented this also and inspired me to find it otherwise.

[71] This temptation was stronger than the
former, inasmuch as it went to the innermost, and
on the other side I had stronger proof of the spirit;
for I sometimes burst out into a sweat. That which
was suggested was not at all as if it would condemn
me more, for I had the strong assurance that this
was forgiven me; but it was that I should excuse
myself, and make myself free. I burst frequently into
tears, not from sorrow, but from inward rejoicing
that our Lord had chosen to show so unworthy a
sinner such great grace; for I found from it all that
this was the sum; that the only thing is to cast
oneself with humility into our Lord's grace, to find
one's own unworthiness, and thank God in humility
for his grace; for if any glorification is in it, which
makes for one's own honor, be it glorification of
God's grace or whatever else, it is to this extent
impure.

[72] When, as was often the case, I was in my
thoughts about these very subjects, and anyone
accounted me as a holy man and on this account
offered me dignity—as indeed it happens among
certain simple people that they not only venerate
but even adore some supposedly holy man as a
saint—I then found that in the earnestness which
then possessed me, I desired to do him all the ill I
could to the highest degree, in order that nothing at
all of the sin should stick to him, and that with

earnest prayers I ought to appease our Lord, in order that I might never have any part of so damning a sin to stick to me. [73] For Christ, in whom all the Godhead is perfect, ought alone to be prayed to; for he takes the greatest sinners to grace and regards as nothing our unworthiness; how can we therefore address ourselves in prayer to other than to him? He is almighty and the only mediator, which he does for other's sake; the holy are made such; it is his work, and not ours, that we should...[The three last words are crossed out. *Editor*]

[74] I found myself more unworthy than others and the greatest of sinners, as our Lord has permitted me to go deeper into certain things with my thoughts than many other people; and the very fountain of sin lies there, in the thoughts, which are carried out in action; which in this way causes my sins to have come from a deeper ground than many other people's. Therein I found my own unworthiness, and my sins greater than other men's. For it is not enough to make oneself out to be unworthy, which may consist of something from which the heart is far away, and may be a counterfeit; but to find out the fact that one is unworthy belongs to the grace of the spirit.

[75] Now while I was in the spirit, I thought and sought how I might by my thoughts attain the knowledge of how to avoid all that was impure; still I marked, notwithstanding, that the impure, on all occasions, put itself forward. I found that it was

dwelt upon in thought from the point of view of self love. For instance, if any person did not regard me according to the estimate of my own imagination, I discovered that I always thought to myself, "Ah! if you only knew what grace I have, you would act otherwise." This was at once impure, and had self love for its basis. At last I found this out, and prayed to God for his forgiveness. And then I asked that others might enjoy the same grace; which perhaps they had, or do receive. Thus I could here clearly observe in myself one more of the horrible apples still remaining, entirely unconverted, which are the root of Adam, and original sin. Nay, and endless other roots of sin belong to me besides.

[76] I heard a person sitting at table propose to his neighbor the question whether anybody could be melancholy who had a superabundance of money. I laughed in my own mind, and I felt inclined to answer, if it had been right to do so in that company or if the question had been put to me, that a person who has all means in excess is not only subject to melancholy but to melancholy in a higher place, in the state of the mind and the soul, or the spirit which operates therein. Wondered that he raised such a question. [77] I can the better testify of this, as by God's grace I have received as my portion a superabundance of all I want in worldly

means, can live in plenty on my annual income,[32] and carry out the plans I have in my mind; and put by something after all. I can thus bear my testimony that the misery and the melancholy which arise from lack of life's necessities are low in degree and bodily in pressure, but are by no means so bad as the other kind. But as the power of the Spirit is in the one, the other knows nothing of this, for it may seem as if the former were strong so far as the body is concerned; but into this I do not enter.

[The last sentence from "But as" is crossed out with a thick stroke, made immediately after it was written.]

[78] Saw a bookseller's shop. Thought immediately that my works would do more than other people's. But then it struck me at once that one is servant to another, and our Lord has among his means a thousand issues for preparing one man; and thus every book ought to be left to its own value, as a means near or remote according to the state of each man's reason. Still, pride, arrogance will push forth; may God control it, who has the power in his hands.

[79] Had so much of the Lord's grace that when I would determine to keep my thoughts in purity I found I had an inward joy, but still a torment in the

---

[32]According to the estimate of his friend Cuno of Amsterdam, Swedenborg had an annual income of about 10,000 florins or 5196 Swedish dalers in copper. (See Tafel *Doc.* II, page 447.)

body, which could not at all bear the heavenly joy of the soul: for I left myself most humbly in God's grace, to do with me according to his pleasure. God grant me humility, that I may see my own weakness, uncleanness, and unworthiness.

[80][33] During all this time I was in society as usual and no one could in the least [observe in me any change]; this was of God's grace; but I knew what the case was, not daring to say that so high grace had been vouchsafed me; for I found that it would conduce to no end, but for people to think about me in one way or another, for or against, each person in his own way. I found that it could do no good were I to mention in private society, for the alleged glorification of God's grace, that which might redound to my *amour propre*.

[81] I found no better comparison for myself than when a peasant is raised to power as a chief or king and can command all that his heart desired; but who yet had something in him that caused him to wish to learn that of which he himself knew nothing. And from the comparison one discovers that it is...thy gracious hand that causes the great joy. Yet

---

[33]On page 29 of the original manuscript (see Phototype Volume XVIII of the Swedenborg MSS., pp 618ff) there are only twenty lines of writing and these were crossed and blotted out with ink. After much labor, the original Swedish editor managed to decipher a portion of the writing.

was I sorrowing to think that man can by no means place himself within that grace.

[April] 8-9.

[82] It seemed that I had on my knee a dog, and I wondered that it could speak and ask about its former master, Swab;[34] it was blackish, and it kissed me. Wakened, and cried out for Christ's mercy on the great pride I cherish and the self-flattering it induces.

Afterwards I thought that it was my fast day, which had been the day before, and that many things had been packed up for the army.

[83] Afterwards a young woman in dark clothes came in, and told me that I ought to go to...Then there came at my back one that held me so fast, the whole back with the hand and all, that I could not move. I besought one that was beside me for help, and he helped her away; but I had no power to move the arm myself. This was the temptation of the previous day and signifies that I am by no means capable of doing any good thing of myself. Afterwards a whistling was heard as he went away, and I shuddered.

---

[34]This probably refers to Anders Swab (1681-1731), son of Anton Swab of Fahlun and Helena Bergia, the sister of Sarah Bergia, Bishop Swedberg's second wife. See Tafel *Doc.* I, pp. 671-672.

[84] Afterwards I saw in St. Peter's Church a person that went into the chamber underneath where Peter lies, and he was carried out, and it was said that somebody is still lurking there.

It seemed that I was free to go in and out, God lead me.

[85] Afterwards I saw all that was unclean, and recognized myself as unclean, unclean with filth, from head to foot. Cried "Mercy of Jesus Christ."

[A phrase in the Swedish Common Prayer Book, the beginning of the Confession.]

So the thought [of the words] "I, poor sinful man,"[35] was brought before me; which I also read the following day.

[April] 9-10.

[86] The whole day, the ninth, I was in prayer, in songs of praise, in reading God's Word, and fasting; except in the morning, when I was somewhat employed in other matters, until this same temptation came, that I was as it were compelled to think that which I would not.

[87] This night as I was sleeping quite tranquilly, between 3:00 and 4:00 o'clock in the morning, I wakened and lay awake but as in a vision; I could look up and be awake, when I chose, and so I was

---

[35]These are the opening words of the "confession of sins" in the Swedish Liturgy of 1697.

not otherwise than waking; yet in the spirit there was an inward and sensible gladness shed over the whole body; seemed as if it were shown in a consummate manner how it all issued and ended. It flew up, in a manner, and hid itself in an infinitude, as a center. There was love itself. And it seems as though it extended around therefrom, and then down again; thus, by an incomprehensible circle, from the center, which was love, around, and so thither again. **[88]** This love, in a mortal body, whereof I then was full, was like the joy that a chaste man has at the very time when he is in actual love and in the very act with his mate; such extreme pleasantness was suffused over the whole of my body, and this for a long time, lasting all the interval of waking, especially just before I went off to sleep, and after sleep, half an hour or an hour. Now while I was in the spirit, and still awake for I could open my eyes, and be awake, and then again enter the state, I saw and observed that the inward and actual joy came from this source, and that in so far as any one could be therein, so much cheer has he; and so soon as any one comes into another love that does not concentrate itself thither, so soon he is out of the way; **[89]** for instance when he came into any love for himself—to any that did not center there—then he was outside of the way. There came a little chill over me and a sort of slight shiver as if it tortured me. From this I found from what my troubles had sometimes arisen, and then I found whence the great anguish comes when the spirit afflicts a man; and that it, at last, ends in everlasting torment and has hell for its portion, when a man unworthily partakes of Christ in the Holy Supper; for it is the Spirit that torments the man for his unworthiness. **[90]** In the same condition in which I was, I came yet deeper into the spirit, and although I was awake, I could by no means govern myself, but there came a kind of overmastering tendency to throw myself upon my face, to clasp my hands, and to pray as before; to pray for my unworthiness, and with the deepest humility and reverence to pray for grace; that I, as the greatest of sinners, might have the forgiveness of sins. Then also I observed that I was in the same state as the night before last; but could tell nothing further, because I was awake.

[91] At this I wondered; and so it was shown me in the spirit that man in this state is as a man with his feet upwards and his head downwards. And it came before me why Moses had to put off his shoes when he was to go to the holy place, and why Christ washed the apostles' feet, and answered Peter that when the feet are washed all is done. Afterwards in the spirit I found that that which goes out from the very center, which is love, is the Holy Spirit, which is represented by water; for it is called water or wave.

[92] In fine, when a man is in the condition of having no love that centers in himself but that

centers only in the general or public good, which
represents here on earth in the moral world the love
in the spiritual world, and this not at all for his own
sake or society's sake but for Christ's sake, in whom
love is and center is, then is man in the right state.
Christ is ultimate end, the other ends are mediate
ends; they lead direct to the ultimate end.

[93] Afterwards I fell into sleep, and saw one of
my acquaintances at a table; he saluted me, but I
did not observe it at once or return his salutation;
he was angry and gave me some hard words. I tried
to excuse myself, and at last I said that I was liable
to be buried in thought and not to observe it when
any one saluted me, so that sometimes I passed my
friends in the street without seeing them. I appealed
in confirmation of this to another acquaintance who
was present, and he said it was so; and I said that
no one wished to be (God grant this may be so)
more polite and humble than I. This dream happened on account of the former night when I was in
other thoughts than I ought to have entertained,
and it showed that our Lord in his infinite mercy is
willing to excuse me. But my friend made no reply
thereto; however he seemed to be convinced, as I
believed.

[April] 10-11.

[94] Came into a low room where there were
many people; saw however only one woman, was in

black, but not evil; she walked a long way into a bedroom, but I would not go with her. She waved to me at the door. Afterwards I went out and found myself detained several times by a specter which held me all down the back. At last it disappeared, [95] and I came out. Came a foul specter which did the same thing: it was a foul old man. At last I got away from them. It was my thoughts that I had had the day before when I regarded myself as all too unworthy and thought that in my lifetime I should never surmount this state; but yet consoled myself with the thought that God is mighty in all things, and that his power does it; yet still there was something in me that caused me not to submit myself as I ought to God's grace, to do with me according to his good pleasure.

[96] When I came out, I saw a great many people sitting in a gallery, and lo! a mighty stream of water came down through the roof; it was so mighty that it broke through all that it met. There were some that barred the opening or hole. Some also that went aside so that the water should not hit them. Some that dissipated it into drops. Some that diverted its course so that it turned away from the stand. This, I suppose, was the power of the Holy Spirit that flowed into the body and the thoughts, and which in part I impeded; in part I went out of its way; in part, I slanted it from me. For the people I saw represent my thoughts and will.

[97] Afterwards I came out of this and was enabled in my thoughts in a certain way to measure and divide into parts that which went from center to circumference. It seemed to be heaven; for there was afterwards a heavenly brightness. I can indeed have my thoughts about this; but as yet I dare not be too confident; because it concerns something that is to happen.

[98] While I was in the first struggle of this trial, I cried to Jesus for help, and it went away. I also held my hands together under my head, and in this manner it did not return the second time. Yet when I awoke, I had shiverings and I heard time after time a heavy muffled sound, but did not know whence it came.

[99] Afterwards, when I was awake, I wondered to myself whether this might not be phantasm. Then I observed that my faith faltered; but I prayed with clasped hands that I might be strengthened in the faith, and this immediately took place. My own worthiness in comparison with others also came into my head; prayed as before; and the thought of it disappeared at once. So that if our Lord takes his hand from one in the very least, one is out of the right way, and the true faith, as it was with me, according to this very palpable showing.

[100] I slept about eleven hours this night, and all the morning was in my usual state of inward joy; yet there was a pang with it. This I supposed to arise from the power of the spirit and my own unworthiness. At last by God's assistance I attained to the thought that man ought to be satisfied with all that the Lord pleases, for it is his; and that man does not at all resist the spirit when he obtains from God the assurance that it is God's grace as it works for our good; for as we are his, so we must be content with what it pleases him to do with that which is his. For this however man ought to pray to our Lord, for it does not in the very least come within our own power.

[101] He then gave me his grace to this end: I passed a little inward with my thoughts, and wanted to understand wherefore it happened so; which was a sin. The thoughts had no right there; but I ought to pray our Lord for ability to govern them. It is enough that he so pleases. But in everything one ought to call upon, to pray to, and to thank him; and with humility to acknowledge our own unworthiness.

[102] Still I am weak in body and in thought, for I know of nothing but my own unworthiness and that I am a miserable creature, which torments me. And by this I see how unworthy I am of the grace that has been granted me.

[103] Observed also that the stream, as it fell down, pierced through the clothes of a person who was sitting there as he was stepping out of the way. Perhaps a drop has fallen upon me, and presses hard; what would it be if the whole stream came.

For I adopted the motto:

> God's will be done: I am thine and not mine
> [struck out] God gives grace thereto; this
> is by no means mine.

[104] I discovered that a man may be in spiritual agony although he is assured by the spirit that he has obtained the forgiveness of sins; and has the hope and the assurance of being in God's grace. This may [the two last words are crossed out].

[April] 11-12.

[105] I was dreaming the whole night, though only the smallest fraction of it comes to mind. It was as if I was being taught all night in many things of which I have no recollection. I was asleep about eleven hours. So far as I can recall it, I think (1) it was the said substantials or essentials which a man ought to study and investigate. (2) It was told me also of the thymus and renal gland [of which he was then writing in *Regnum Animale*][36] that as the thymus separates the impure serum from the blood, and the renal gland carries it back into the blood after it has been purified, so it also happens in us, as I believe, spiritually.

---

[36]Vol. II, n. 379.

[106] (3) It seems that I saw my sister Caisa,[37] who did something somewhat amiss and afterwards lay down and cried out. When our mother came she assumed a totally different mien and a different speech, the signification of which shall be given hereafter. **[107]** (4) There was a priest who preached to a great congregation, and at the end spoke against another person, but whether he was named or not I do not know. But then one stepped up and talked against him and said that it ought not to be so. I was with them afterwards in a private company, and then, on inquiry, it was said that the punishment for such a matter is disgrace, with a fine of three marks Swedish. He seemed to be not at all aware that it was thus punishable. It was said that one begins with what costs one mark, then two marks, etc.; which signifies that a man ought not to preach against anyone, or to speak, or to write; for it is punishable and slanderous in the eye of the law. For it touches one's honor and good name. **[108]** (5) Afterwards my knees were moved of themselves, which may signify that I had been somewhat humiliated, as also is the case; which is God's grace, for which I am most humbly thankful.

[109] Afterwards I found in myself, and perhaps was directed to it by the third point in the dream, that in every one of our thoughts, yea in that

---

[37]A nickname for Catharina, Swedenborg's sister. See family table in Tafel *Doc.* I, pp. 83-84.

thought that we believe almost pure, there adheres an endless amount of sin and impurity; as also in every desire that comes from the body into the thoughts, which spring originally from very great roots. Although thought should appear to be pure, yet underneath it is the fact that the man thinks from fear, from hypocrisy, and many other passions; as indeed one may somewhat discover by reflection; so that we can all the less make ourselves free from sin, in that there is no thought that is not mingled with much uncleanness or impurity. Therefore it is best every hour and moment to confess oneself guilty of hell punishment; but to believe that the grace and mercy of God, which is in Jesus Christ, overlooks it. **[110]** Yes, I have often observed that the whole of our will that we have got, that is ruled of the body, and that introduces thoughts, is opposed to the spirit which does this. Therefore there is a continual fight, and we cannot in any way unite ourselves to the spirit; but the spirit, of grace, unites with us. On this account we are as it were dead to all that is good; but we can incline ourselves to the bad. For a man ought always to count himself guilty of numerous sins; for the Lord God knows all (and we, very little) of our sins that only come into our thoughts; [we know] only of those that come into our actions, when we become persuaded of their sinfulness.

It is also to be noticed [crossed out].

[April] 12-13.

[111] I observed through the spirit that I was in the same mental state that I had been the day before; which was also represented to me by a kind of spiritual light-writing; that the will influences the understanding most in inspiration [breathing in]. The thoughts then fly out of the body inward, and in expiration are as it were driven out, or carried straight forth; showing that the very thoughts have their alternate play like the respiration of the lungs;[38] because inspiration belongs to the will, expiration to nature. Thus the thoughts have their play in every act of respiration; therefore when evil thoughts entered, the only thing to do was to draw to oneself the breath; so the evil thoughts vanished. [112] Hence one may also see the reason that during strong thought the lungs are held in equilibrium, still more in a condition of nature; and at this time the inspirations go quicker than the expirations; at other times the reverse is the case. Also, of the fact that in ecstasy or trance the man holds his breath; at this time the thoughts are, in a manner of speaking, away. Likewise in sleep, when both inspiration and expiration belong to nature; when that is represented which flows in from a higher source. The same may also be deduced from

---

[38]See *Regnum Animale*, vol II, n. 410. See also Tafel *Doc.* II, p. 175.

the cerebrum; because in inspiration all the organs intimate with the cerebrum itself are expanded; and the thoughts then obtain their origin and their course.

[113] Afterwards I came to a place where wondrously large and high windmills were turning with dreadful rapidity. Then I came into a darkness, and I crept upon the ground and was afraid that one of the sails of the windmills would lay hold of me and kill me. I actually got beneath a sail, which then stopped, and I was well off with it; for the sail helped me. This signifies that the day before I was in combat with my thoughts (which are meant by the sails of the windmills) and meantime I had no idea what I should do; but with God's assistance my thoughts were tempered and so I was brought away safe and sound. Wherefore, honor and praise to God who does not despise my weakness.

[114] Afterwards I seemed to be in company with some who endeavored as it were to make gold; but they saw that they must climb up; but this they could not do, and without it, it was impracticable to make gold. This went on for a time; then at last I was with two persons who attempted in spite of all to rise up; although our Lord was by no means with them. I said: It cannot possibly be done; and so I went up before them. I had a rope, and pulled. Observed that underneath there was something that pulled strongly the other way. At last I saw it was a fellow, whom I had the better of, and lifted him up;

and so I congratulated myself, and said that it was as I had said. [115] Signification I believe is this: the gold signifies what is good and pleasing to God; one must climb up to get it; and this is by no means within the compass of our own power, however much we imagine that by our own powers we are able to do it; but then we find that there is that which pulls forcibly the other way; however at last we conquer through God's grace.

[116] Afterwards I was for a considerable time in the same thought, which became ruddy in its light, which ruddiness signifies that therein is God's grace, and that upon this depends the issue of our really doing (with God's grace and in faith, which may God give) that which is good. This is making gold; for in this case man gets from our Lord all that is wanted, all that is useful to him. Thus was represented very powerfully that that which is good ought to be effected, and that the gold lies therein.

[117] Afterwards when I had risen up I was in a great fear before our Lord as in a chill; the least intimation or thought that frightened me made me shiver; which was God's grace to show me that I must seek salvation with fear and trembling. And as it is my motto, "Thy will be done; I am thine, and not mine"; and as I have given myself from myself to our Lord; so let him do with me according to his good pleasure. And in the body also there was a certain dissatisfaction; but in the spirit, gladness

thereat; for it is our Lord's grace that does it. God strengthen me therein.

[118] Was continually in a fight with double thoughts that battled against each other. I pray thee, O Almighty God, that I may obtain the grace to be thine and not mine. Forgive me if I have said that I am thine and not mine; this is not my province; it is God's. I pray for the grace to be able to be thine, and that in nought I be left to myself.

[April] 13-14.

[119] Thought how the grace of the Spirit the whole night worked with me. Saw my sister Hedwig,[39] with whom I would have nothing to do; which signifies that I ought on no account to busy myself with the *Oeconomia Regni Animalis* but to leave it.[40] Afterwards it seemed to me when time hung heavy, she first said to her children: Go out and read: afterwards, that we might play drafts, or cards, and they sat down to these to pass away the time. It seemed then I was at dinner. I believe it signifies

---

[39]See Tafel *Doc.* I, pp. 83-84. See also *S.D.* nn. 5134, 5702, 5883.

[40]It is uncertain what this means. The *Oeconomia* was completed and published in 1740-41. Odhner suggests it may refer to the method followed in that work. Swedenborg may, of course, have intended to write *Regnum Animale*.

that there is nothing wrong or criminal when one does this in the right way.

[120] Lay with one that was by no means pretty, but still I liked her. She was made like others; I touched her there, but found that at the entrance it was set with teeth. It seemed that it was Archenholtz[41] in the guise of a woman. What it means I do not know; either that I am to have no commerce with women; or that in politics lies that which bites; or something else.

[121] The whole day I was in double thought that tried to destroy the spiritual as it were with scoffing, so that I found the temptation very strong. Through the grace of the Spirit I was brought to fasten my thoughts on a tree, then upon Christ's cross and on Christ crucified. As often as I did this, the other thoughts as of themselves fell flat. [122] I pressed with the same thought so forcibly that I seemed with the cross to press down the tempter and drive him away. Then I was for a time free, and afterwards I had to hold my thoughts so fixed on this that whenever I lost this out of my thoughts and inward sight I fell into tempting thoughts. God be praised, who gave me the weapon. God of his grace maintain me therein, that I always may have my

---

[41]Johan Archenholtz (1695-1777) was a Swedish politician and historian and a leader of the "Caps" party at the Swedish Diet. Like his political ally Swedenborg, he opposed the 1741 declaration of war against Russia.

crucified savior before my eyes; for I dared by no
means look upon my Jesus, him that I have seen;
for I am an unworthy sinner; but rather I ought to
fall upon my face; and Jesus it is that takes me up
to look upon him; for thus I am enabled to look
upon Christ crucified.

[April] 14-15.

[123] It seemed that I ran fast down some steps,
but only slightly touched each step as I passed,
coming fortunately all the way down without peril.
A voice came from my dear father: "You are creating
alarm, Emanuel." He said it was wicked, but that he
would overlook it. It meant that yesterday I had
made too bold a use of Christ's cross; yet it was
God's grace that I came free of danger.

[124] So I climbed up on a shelf, and struck the
neck off a bottle, from which there flowed a thick
stuff and covered the floor. Then it flowed downwards, I believe. Means that with God's grace and
no power of mine a mass of evil was rooted out
yesterday from my thoughts. Sat upon something
that was written on, meaning what I still have to do.

[125] Heard a bear growl but did not see him.
Did not dare to stay in the upper story, for there
was a dead body there that he would smell. I
therefore went down to the apartment of Doctor

Moraeus,[42] and closed the shutters. This betokens temptation, both on the score of covetousness and perhaps of other things; also that I am pursuing my anatomical speculations.

[126] It seemed to me that Doctor Moraeus paid court to a pretty girl, obtained her consent, and thus had the means of taking her where he chose. I joked with her about the readiness with which she said "Yes;" etc., etc. She was a pretty girl, and grew bigger and prettier. It meant that I should inform myself about the muscles[43] and reflect upon them.

[127] I had a preternaturally good and long sleep for twelve hours. When I wakened I had Jesus crucified and his cross before my eyes. The spirit came with its heavenly life, as it were ecstatic, intense; and in a manner allowed me to go higher and higher in that state so that had I gone on higher, I should have been dissolved away by this same actual life of joy.

[128] It came thus before me in the spirit that I had gone too far; that I in my thoughts had embraced Christ on the cross. Then I kissed his feet and afterwards removed myself away; then falling upon my knees I prayed to him crucified. It seemed that as often as I did this, the sins of my weakness

---

[42]Cf. *S.D.* n. 4717. Moraeus was Swedenborg's cousin.

[43]See *Regnum Animale* II, nn. 449-453. See also Tafel *Doc.* II, p. 179, note.

were forgiven. It came to me that I could have the same thing before the eyes of my body in an image; but this I found was far from right, and was great sin.

[April] 15-16.

[129] It seemed that I climbed up a ladder out of a great deep; after me came...(women) whom I knew. I stood still and frightened them, on purpose, and then I went up. Came against a green wall, and lay down. The others came after. I saluted them. They were women. They laid down side by side with me; a young woman, and one a little older. I kissed both their hands and did not know at all which I should have. It was my thoughts and my *ouvrage d'esprit*, of two kinds, which at last came up with me; I regained and saluted them, and received them.

[130] Afterwards I came to a place where a great many men folks were assembled, a large number of handsome young people in one place in a group. Fresh ones came up, for instance, Henning Gyllenborg,[44] on horseback; I went up and kissed him and stood beside him. Signifies that I return to my *res memoria*, and *res imaginationis:* my cherished

---

[44]Count Henning Adolph Gyllenborg (1715-1775), politician and diplomat, was a leader of the "Hats" and finally Councilor of State.

objects of memory and imagination, and salute them once again; therefore I came again to the higher and the lower faculty.[45]

[131] After I came home and was at home in my own house, many came to me. I knew I had hidden a pretty little woman and a boy, and I kept them hidden. For the rest there were few provisions for such a company. But I was not yet willing to display my silver, before I had to entertain them; nor yet to conduct them into an inner magnificent apartment which was finely embellished within. It signifies that I came home to myself again, and that I had won the knowledge that is now written down,[46] and that in time I may be enabled to make use thereof, and to set forth the silver, and to carry the people into the elegant bedroom.

[132] It seemed that I accused somebody, but do not remember how; but at last I smoothed the matter down and somewhat excused it because he himself said it was so; but the words were buried deep. Signifies that I accused myself, but nevertheless excused myself, because I myself confessed all.

[133] It was said, *Nicolaiter*, and *Nicolaus Nicolai;* whether it can mean my new name, I do not know.

---

[45]See Epilogue to Part II of *Regnum Animale*, Vol. II, pp. 331-366, especialy note (*l*), p. 348. See also Tafel *Doc.* II, p. 180.

[46]See Tafel *Doc.* II, p. 180, note.

The most remarkable thing was this, that I now represented the inner man and was as another person than myself, so that I made salutation to my own thoughts, frightening them; saluted my own stores of memory; accused another person; which shows that the change has come; that I represent one who is against another; that is to say, the inner man, for I have prayed God that I in no wise may be mine but that God may be pleased to let me be his.

This has now lasted for twenty-one days.

[134] I found furthermore that the most of this has a signification of another kind. (1) The two women meant that I should rather be in philosophical studies than in spiritual ones; which soon revealed my inclination. (2) My kissing Henning Gyllenborg and seeing so many people showed that I was not only pleased with the power of being in the world but that I also liked to boast of my work. (3) Nicolaus Nicolai was a philosopher who every year sent bread to Augustus; meant debts, that I found my duty to be again reconciled to our Lord, because I, in spiritual things, am a stinking corpse. [135] For I went to the envoy, Preis, and he went to Pastor Pambo to ask him if I could take the Holy Supper afresh, which was granted me; I met him at the envoy's, and went in with him. This was our

Lord's providence. I dined the same day with Envoy Preis,[47] but had no appetite.

The 17th, was at the Lord's Supper with Pastor Pambo.[48]

[April] 17-18.

[136] Hideous dreams: how the executioner roasted the head he had struck off; and laid one roast head after the other in an empty oven that never got full. It was said that it was his meat. He was a great big woman; smiled; had a little girl with him.

[137] Afterwards the Wicked One carried me into sundry deeps and bound me. I do not remember it all. Was cast bound all over into hell.

[138] How a great procession was arranged, from which I was excluded. I ought to have departed from it; but I could go there; sat myself down; but they advised me to go away. I went. Still, I had another room from which I was able to see them. But still the procession had not yet come.

---

[47]Joachim Fredrik Preis (1667-1759) was Swedish Envoy at The Hague. Swedenborg greatly admired Ambassador Preis and called on him often. See letters from Swedenborg to Preis in *New Church Life*, 1896, pp. 186 and 186. See also *Letters & Memorials*, vol. 1, pp. 256, 258, 486, 499.

[48]Pastor Johann Gottlieb Pambo was minister of the German Lutheran church at The Hague in 1744. See *New Church Life*, 1914, p. 766.

[139] Still, as I am sure that God exercises grace and compassion to all poor sinners who desire to be converted and with a steady faith fly to his inconceivable mercifulness and to the merits of the Savior, Jesus Christ, so I make myself sure of his grace and leave myself in his protection, because I believe certainly that I have obtained pardon of my sins; which is my trust and consolation, which may God for Jesu Christ's sake strengthen.

[140] Was this day at intervals in inward suffering and sometimes in despair; still, was assured of the forgiveness of sins. In this state stood hard combat from time to time till 10 o'clock, when with God's help I fell into a sleep in which it seemed that it was said to me that something was about to be offered from within. Slept for one and one-half hours, though in the night I had slept more than ten hours. Have had by God's grace preternatural sleep; as also for the whole of the half year.[49]

[April] 18-19.

[141] It seemed to me that we worked long to bring in a chest, in which were contained precious things which had long lain there; just as it was a long work with Troy;[50] at last, one went in under-

---

[49]See Tafel *Doc.* II, note 168, pp. 1118-1127.

[50]Possibly a reference to the Trojan horse.

neath and eased it onwards; it was thus gotten in as conquered; and we sawed and sawed. Signifies how a man shall work in order to win heaven.

[142] It seemed that I had a bad watch[51] with me, but valuable watches at home, which I would by no means exchange for gold watches. Signifies that I learn few knowledges that are noble enough to spend my time on.

[143] I seemed to myself in the lower parts to be enveloped in lamellated strata that in various ways were entwined about me, and at the same moment came as it were...Signifies that I should take further care to continue in the right end.

[144] There was a very good natured dog, dark brown, that followed me; when any reptile or vermin came, he rose up; when there was water, he went there in order to know the depth. Perhaps it signifies Tobias' dog.[52]

[145] Saw a wonderful beast in a window; it was lively; also dark brown; and it went in through another window; and that which was upon its back was scrubbed off and turned into a pocket handkerchief. I looked after him, and saw him still a little; but could not point him out to another; in this window there was a chemist's shop. I asked if I should shoot him. It may perhaps mean that I shall

---

[51]See Tafel *Doc.* II, p. 609.

[52]See the Book of Tobit, 6:1.

be instructed about whatever serves for amendment, etc.

[146] Thought afterwards that it was shown, that it was said to me, or is intended to be understood, when I went astray.

[147] I saw König and Professor Winbom[53] coming, that is to say, I came to stay with them; on week days with those that are by no means Christians; for König was said to be no Christian. Winbom came on foot, which means Sundays.

[148] This day I was also somewhat uneasy in my mind because the thoughts flew against my will one way and another, and I could not hold them in. I was in divine service and found that the thoughts on matters of faith—about Christ, his merits, and the like—in so far as they are on the right side and confirming nevertheless cause unrest and let loose and let forth contrary thoughts, which a man can by no means parry when he wills to believe of his own understanding and not of the Lord's grace.

[149] In the end it was given me of the Spirit's grace to obtain faith without reasoning, an assurance about it. Then I saw my thoughts that confirmed it, as it were under me; I laughed in my mind at them, and much more at those that rebutted them and were contrary. The faith seemed to

---

[53]Anders Winbom (1687-1745) was a gifted and popular professor of moral theology at Uppsala.

be far above my understanding's thoughts. Then first I got peace; God strengthen me therein; for it is his work, and so much the less mine, as my thoughts, yea even the best, more destroy than advance or nourish it. A man laughs at himself, both when he thinks against and also when he would confirm with his understanding that which he believes. It is therefore the higher thing, I do not at all know if it is not the highest, when a man gets the grace of no longer using his understanding in matters of faith: **[150]** although it would appear that our Lord with certain persons allows assurance to proceed from considerations that concern the understanding. Happy are they that believe and do not see. This I have clearly written in the Prologue, n. 21, 22.[54] But still of myself I could by no means have remembered this, or arrived thereat; but God's grace, me unknowing, worked it. Then I afterwards, from the fact and the change in all my inward being, found it; for it is God's grace and work, to which be eternal honor. **[151]** I see herefrom how difficult it is for the learned, far more difficult than for the unlearned, to come to this faith; and thus to overcome themselves so that they can laugh at themselves; for adoration of their own understanding must in the very first place be plucked up and cast down; which is God's work and not man's. So

---

[54]*Regnum Animale.*

likewise it is God's work to maintain a man in this state. This faith becomes thus separated from our understanding, and sits ever above it.

[152] This is pure faith; the other is impure, so long as it mixes itself up with our understanding; it ought to take its understanding captive, under obedience to faith. The man's belief ought therefore to rest upon this: he that has said it is God, who is over all, the truth itself. That is, as we may understand it, that we ought to be as children. A good part of what I have seen harmonizes with this, and perhaps this also, that so many heads were roasted, and thrown into the oven, to form the food of the Evil One.

[153] The fact that confirmations darken faith is also seen hereby, that in this case the understanding never goes beyond probabilities. In this mode there always lurks as it were the proving of the greater or the lesser; for the confirmations of one's own understanding are always subject to doubt, which darkens the light of faith. But thus faith is only God's gift, which man obtains if he lives according to God's commands and thus assiduously prays to him for it.

[April] 19-20.

[154] Had quite a different sleep; dreamt much: after which I had shiverings, but could not bring

back any of it to mind, for every time the dreams vanished from me.

[155] I held my hands together. In the act of waking it seemed to me that they were pressed together by a hand or finger; which with God's help signifies that our Lord heard my prayers.

[156] Afterwards in a vision (which is not sleep, not waking, not ecstasy) it came to me that King Charles battled the first time with a vain result; afterwards in the second battle with the Saxons won the victory, and was covered with blood. Afterwards again that the Muses have won. Which signifies that with God's grace I have won the fight, and that Jesus' blood and merits helped me, and that I in my studies shall win my end.

[157] I rose up now a whole God up;[55] to God be thanks and praise; *I will not at all be my own. I am sure and I believe that thou, O God, lettest me be thine in all the days of my life and takest not thy Holy Spirit from me, that strengthens and upholds me.*

[158] This day I was in the strongest temptation so that when I thought on Jesus Christ there came in at once therewith godless thoughts, which I had no power of controlling as far as I could know. I struck myself; but I can affirm that I never had felt

---

[55]The meaning of this is not clear. Tafel rendered it, "I then arose, full of God."

such lively courage as this day, not in the smallest degree cast down, timorous or hurt as on other days; although the temptation was the strongest, the cause being that our Lord had given me the strong faith and confidence, that he helps me for Jesus Christ's sake and his promise, so that I then found out the work of faith.

[159] And the case with this courage was that I was so angry with satan that I would fight with him with the weapons of faith. From this we find what is the effect of a right faith, without reasoning, or support by reasons.

But it is God's grace alone; had it happened before, I should have been altogether abashed. I was however afraid that I had offended our Lord with forcibly trying to free myself, for which however with humility to the best of my power I besought forgiveness. It may possibly have reference to Charles XII, who was bloody all over.

[April] 21-22.

[160] It seemed that I went wandering astray in the darkness and did not go out with the others. I felt my way along the walls and came at last out into a beautiful house in which there were people who were puzzled as to how I could come this way. They met me and said that this is not the way. I said that in the garret there may be an opening into here. They said, "No." Signifies that I went woefully wrong this day.

[161] And there was a large dog that got under the bed spread where I lay and licked me on the neck. I was afraid he would bite me, but nothing of the kind occurred, and it was said he would not bite me. Signifies the double thoughts[56] I had had, and that I was barred from thinking on holy things.

[162] Afterwards I was with players. One said that a Swede was come who wished to see me. We drove in. A large ladder was set for him. It was a dog enveloped round, with a whelp that sucked it. It signifies my horrid thoughts. Something of the same kind hung from a fishing rod and would not go away. At last, in another room, it was torn away. Signifies that I became free therefrom.

[163] In vision it seemed to me as if something were torn asunder in the air. It may perhaps betoken that my double thoughts should be torn asunder.

When I wakened there was heard the phrase, *all grace*; which signifies that all that has happened is grace and for my good.

[164] Afterwards I came into doubt because I seemed to be widely separated from God, so as not to be able to think about him so vividly, unless I turn my course home. There came a number of

---

[56]See *S.D.* n. 484.

involved motions of the soul and the body, but I took courage, and found that I am come to do the best of all and to promote God's honor; got the talent; all helped thereto. The Spirit was with me from youth to this end. I held myself unworthy to live if I do other than go the right way; and so laughed at the other seducing thoughts.

[165] So as to luxury, riches, station, which I had pursued. All this I found to be vanity, and that he is happier who has none of it in possession but is contented than he who has it. For I laughed at all reasons that confirmed, and thus with God's help resolved myself, God help.

It seemed that a hen cackled, as happens directly after she lays an egg.

[166] Furthermore I perceived that faith, in fact, consists in a sure confidence one gets from God, but yet consists in the work that one does in doing what is good to his neighbor, each according to his talent, and this more and more; and that one does it of faith that God so commanded and does not reason any further about it, but does love's work under obedience to faith; even though it were against the body's pleasure and against the body's persuasions. So therefore a faith without deeds is no right faith. A man must actually forsake himself.

[April] 22-23.

[167] Troublesome dreams, about dogs who were said to be my countrymen, and who sucked my neck, but did not bite it; moreover, what I intended to do with two persons, but nothing came of it. In the morning I fell into horrid thoughts, as on the day before, that the Evil One had got me; yet with the assurance that he was outside, and soon would let me go. **[168]** When I was in damnable thoughts, the worst that could be, in the same hour Jesus Christ was presented strongly before my inner eyes and the operation of the Holy Spirit came over me, so that I could know therefrom that the devil was away. The next day I was from time to time in combat and in double thoughts and strife; after dinner I was in very pleasant spirits, and thought of God, although I was in a mundane condition; I was then travelling to Leiden.

[April] 23-24. In Leiden.

[169] It seemed that I fought with a woman in flight, who drove me down into the lake, and up; at last, I struck her on the forehead as hard as possible with a plate and bore down upon her face, until she appeared to be got the better of. It was my struggles and my combat with my thoughts which I had overcome.

[170] It seemed to me it was said that he grows more internal, he is completing; which signifies that through my struggles I was inwardly cleansed.

[171] Afterwards during the whole night something holy was dictated to me, which ended with *"sacrarium et sanctuarium."* I found myself lying in bed with a woman, and said, "Had you not used the word *sanctuarium,* we would have done it." I turned away from her. She with her hand touched my member, and it grew large, larger than it ever had been. I turned round and applied myself; it bent, yet it went in. She said it was long. I thought during the act that a child must come of it; and it succeeded *en merveille.*

There was one beside the bed who lurked about afterwards; but she went away first.

[172] This denotes the uttermost love for the holy; for all love has its origin therefrom; is a series; in the body it consists in its actuality in the projection of the seed; when the whole...is there, and is pure, it then means the love for wisdom. The former woman stood for truth; yet as there was one listening, and nothing was done until this one was away, it signifies that we ought to be silent about this matter, and let no one hear of it; because for the worldly understanding it is impure, in itself, pure.

[173] Afterwards I dozed off a little, and it seemed to me that a quantity of oil with some mustard mingled with it was floating about; which perhaps may be my life to come; or it may be satisfaction mixed with calamity; or it may betide some medicine intended for me.

This happened in Leiden on the morning of the 24th of April.

[April] 24-25. In Amsterdam.

[174] During the whole night, for about 11 hours, I was neither asleep nor awake, in a strange trance: knew all that I dreamed; my thoughts were held bound up, which made me sometimes sweat. The state of this sleep I cannot at all describe; but through it my double thoughts were in a manner severed or split asunder. [175] Among other things I dreamed that I talked sometimes with King Charles XII, and he talked away with me, which I wondered at, but in broken French which I did not understand. And when I talked to others, and thought he did not hear, he was close alongside; so that I blushed for what I had said. It means that God speaks with me, and that I understand but the least of it; for it consists of representations, of which as yet I understand very little. Also that he hears and marks everything that is said, and every thought that man has. So also it is sure that no thought escapes his sight, for he sees all to the bottom, ten thousand times more than I myself.

25-26 [Struck out].

[176] It seemed that women and men were set to go away in a ship; and one took hold of my dog,[57] which I took from him. He showed me the way into a beautiful room, where there was some wine. Betokens perhaps that I shall carry my work over to England; and that I should that day be transported thither where I ought to amuse myself; as was in fact the case with Mr. Hinr. Posch. [Pasch?]

[April] 25-26. At The Hague.

[177] A beautiful and precious sleep, for about eleven hours, with various representations: how a woman that was married persecuted me, but I was saved. Signifies that the Lord saves me from temptations and persecutions.

[178] A married woman wished to have me; but my liking was for an unmarried. The former turned against me and persecuted me; but still I attained the unmarried one, and was with her and loved her. Perhaps it meant my thoughts.

[179] There was a woman who had a very fine property, which we walked round, and I was to marry her. She stood for piety and, I believe, wis-

---

[57]The text is uncertain here. It seems to read "min hud" (my skin) rather than "min hund" (my dog). But it is not known if Swedenborg ever had a dog.

dom; she who owned the riches. I went with her also, and loved her after the usual manner; which act appeared to stand for marriage.

[180] So also in a certain way it was represented that I ought not to contaminate myself with other books[58] which concern theological and similar propositions; for this I have in God's Word and from the Holy Spirit.

[April] 28-29.

[181] The night before it seemed I saw King Charles XII, to whom I had formerly dedicated my work;[59] but now I thought he had risen from the dead, and I went out and would now dedicate to him as to any other.

[182] I went along a road; it was a cross road; it was shown me I was to go up; I also went; but thought that I had only some days left; so I went back into the plain: there were many people there; I wished to go out and was pushed very violently.

[183] I gave some fruits to a gardener to sell; he sold them and brought me back two carolines, but said that he retained for himself thirteen dollars; about which I did not trouble myself.

---

[58]See Tafel *Doc.* II, page 260.

[59]Swedenborg had dedicated his *Daedalus Hyperboreus* to the king.

[184] It seemed that I passed my water; a woman in the bed looked at me meanwhile: she was fat and red; I took her afterwards by the bosom; she withdrew herself somewhat; she showed me her secret parts and her obscenity; I declined to have any dealings with her.

[185] All this imports, as it seems to me, that I ought to employ my remaining time upon matters that are higher; and not to write upon worldly themes any more, themes which are comparatively very low; but upon that which regards the very center of all, and indeed, Christ. God be so gracious and enlighten me further about what my duty is; for I am still in some darkness as to whither I should turn.

[186] It seemed that there was one who had written briefly to King Fredrick. He thought it was short; he ordered certain persons to go to him, who at first was a woman, and afterwards a little chap, and in various ways, to bother him with love and such like. They did their best, but I saw that they did not hurt him or do him any harm. He said now, between the 36th and 37th days (which was the day from my temptation) that he will borrow a lot, and go to heaven, and not repay these from whom he has borrowed. I told this to Swab,[60] that he should inform the king of it. All this seems to mean that if

---

[60]See Note 34 above.

I go forward with the other object I proposed to myself, I have borrowed a mass of the spiritual to go to heaven with, which I shall not pay again unless it be at the very last.

[April] 30 - May 1.

[187] I saw one with a sword who was on guard; the sword was pointed and sharp and something stuck upon the coat sleeve. I was in fear because of him; I saw he was somewhat drunk and might do mischief. It means that the day before I had drunk a little more than I ought; which is not of the spirit, but of the flesh, and thus sinful.

[188] Afterwards I had with me Eliezer[61] my deceased brother; so it seemed to me. He was attacked by a wild boar which laid hold of him and bit him. I endeavored to pull the boar down with a hook but could not manage it. Afterwards I went up, and saw him lying between two boars which were eating his head: he had no one to help him; I ran past. It means, as I believe, that the day before I had cared a little too much for a little harlot, and had indulged the appetite of the table, which also is the work of the flesh and not of the spirit; for such

---

[61]Swedenborg's younger brother Eliezer was born in 1692 and died in 1717.

is the life of pigs, which is forbidden by Paul; called by him entertainments.

[189] The day after I watched myself somewhat on this account, but came into a pretty strong trial, in being obliged henceforth in this manner to restrain my appetite; I came into a strange situation and into a kind of chagrin; but yet I was speedily released therefrom, after having prayed and sung a psalm. Rather then I will not be any more mine own, but live as a new man in Christ.

[190] Some days directly after this, I was the greater part of several hours in a spiritual agony, without being able to tell the cause; yet I seemed to myself to be assured of God's grace; however, after dinner I was in a very great state of joyousness and spiritual peace.

[191] When I travelled from The Hague, in the boat from Maasland, it was the 13th of May, it seemed that my brother Jesper[62] was put in prison for my sake; as also another person. I thought I had also put something for which I was answerable in the carriage, and brought it there. The judges came who had to judge him; they had two written papers in their hands. Meantime I saw birds which came flying to me, and I with a pointed knife struck them in the neck so that they died. Afterwards the judges came and set my brother Jesper free; and then I

---

[62]See Tafel *Doc.* I, page 662.

kissed him and rejoiced over him. It means that I have been running wild in my thoughts; but yet with the help of the Spirit have killed them; and that therefore I am proclaimed free.

[192] In Harwich, which was on my arrival in England, I slept only some hours; and then there was shown me much that may perhaps concern my work here. It was the 4th-5th of May, according to the English calendar.[63] [193] 1. How I lost a bank note, and the person who found it got for it only nine stivers;[64] and also another who happened upon a similar note, and it was bought for only nine stivers. And I said in joke that it was sham piety; maybe it means the condition of people in England, which is part honest, part dishonest. [194] 2. There were certain who admired my copper prints, which were well done, and wished to see my rough draft, as if I was able to conceive them just as they were finished. It may mean that my work wins approbation, and they believe that I am not the doer of it. [195] 3. There came to hand a little letter, for which I paid nine stivers. When I opened it there lay within it a great book containing clean blank paper, and among this a great many lovely drawings: the rest, blank paper. There sat a woman on the left

---

[63]The Gregorian calendar (1582) was not adopted in England until 1752.

[64]A "stiver" was a small copper coin of little value.

hand; then she removed to the right and turned over the leaves, and then drawings or designs came forth. It seemed that the meaning of the letter was that I should cause a number of such designs or patterns to be engraved in England. The woman had a rather broad bust and on both sides down to the lower parts was quite bare; the skin, shining as if it were polished; and on the thumb a miniature painting. This may perhaps mean that with God's help while in England I shall be enabled to carry out a number of beautiful designs for my work; and that afterwards speculation may convert herself *ad priora*, which hitherto has been in *posterioribus*; as the alteration from the left to the right seems to suggest. **[196]** 4. It seemed I was commanded to go with Bergen-stjerna[65] on a commission for which the money was provided. It seemed to be all the way to Sicily; and I was well pleased with the commission. But yet I thought it was needful to take care of scorpions. It may perhaps mean something that I may afterwards get among the things committed to me when my work is ready, if haply I am allowed to complete it in another place; and perhaps in some other cause.

[197] May 5-6, in London, I received a blow from a big man, which I took in good part; then I had to

---

[65]Johann Bergenstjerna (1663-1748) was assessor of the College of Mines and a colleague of Swedenborg for many years. In 1735 he married the widow of Eliezer Swedenborg. See *S.D.* nn. 4351, 4396, 5132-3, 5711.

get on a horse to ride at the side of the carriage; but then the horse turned his head round and got me by the head and held me. What it means I do not know. I had to provide myself to some extent against a godly shoemaker[66] who was with me on the road and with whom I lodged at that time. Or was it that I was not thinking of my work?

[198] *Sum of sums.* There is no other thing than grace whereby we are saved. 2. Grace is in Jesus Christ who is the throne of grace. 3. Love to God in Christ is that by which salvation is promoted. 4. And then the man allows himself to be guided by the Spirit of Jesus. 5. All that comes from ourselves is dead, and nothing else than sin; and worthy of everlasting condemnation. 6. For no good can come from any other source than the Lord.

[May] 19-20. In London.

[199] The 20th I was to go to the Lord's Supper in the Swedish Church; but before this, I had fallen into many corrupt thoughts, and I observed that my body continually rebelled; which was also represented to me by scum which had to be taken away. On the morning of the Sunday there came to me through the spirit quite clearly into my mouth, that

---

[66]This refers to a traveling companion of Swedenborg's. See Tafel *Doc.* II, p. 587. See also *The New Church Magazine*, London, Jan. 1914, p. 36.

this is the manna that comes from heaven; it was indeed neither in sleeping nor waking; but quite clearly there came to me in thought and mouth that which signified Christ in the Lord's Supper. The day before I was so set in order that I had inward rest and peace in the Lord's disposal; and also the whole time recognized the Holy Spirit's strong operation, the bliss, and the earthly kingdom of heaven that filled the whole body.

[200] Still I could not at all keep myself under, or hinder myself from seeking after the sex; though I was far from having any intention of committing acts; so that I thought in my dream that it was not so much against God's Ordinance. (I was in company with Prof. Oelreich[67] in certain places.) Of this I was never forewarned, as of other things I had committed. However, that which had been represented to me in a dream some days before happened to me; for in one day I was exposed to two deadly perils; this indeed happened to me, so that had not God then been my protector, I should have given away my life in two places. The particulars I will not describe.

[201] However, the inward joy was so strong and lasting, especially when I was alone by myself,

---

[67]Niklas von Oelreich (1699-1770) was professor of philosophy at Lund, 1732; censor of the press, 1746; president of the College of Commerce, 1767; a leader of the party of "Hats," and, after 1762, of the party of "Caps."

without company, mornings, evenings, days, that it may be likened to heavenly joy here upon earth. This I hope to keep, so long through our Lord's grace alone as I can go the pure way, and have the right view; for if I go aside, and seek my joy in worldly things, it disappears. Whether the inward principle, which is the influx of the spirit of God, is always present is best known to God; however little exultation there may be of which one is conscious. For I thought when I have the heavenly joy why should I seek after the worldly, which in comparison is nothing, is inconstant, harmful, striving against the heavenly and destroying it.

[202] Through various providences I was led to the church which is occupied by the Moravian Brethren,[68] who give themselves out as the true Lutherans and recognize the work of the Holy Ghost, as they tell each other, and only regard God's grace and Christ's blood and merits and simply go to work. More of this at another time; but as yet I am not permitted to join brotherhood with them. Their church was represented to me three months before, just as I have since seen it, and all there were clad like priests.

---

[68]Swedenborg attended the Moravian church in London from time to time. See *The New Church Magazine*, Jan. 1914, p. 34, and Tafel *Doc.* II, p. 587.

June 11-12.

[203] I was in thoughts about those that resisted the Holy Spirit and those that allowed themselves to be governed by it. There appeared to me a man in white with a sword; another went against him, but got wounded by his sword; he again repeated the same attack and now he was run through very badly near the ear and the temples. Again there came another that fought with him; he too was pierced through so that blood was seen. I had a long spear; thought to myself that if he came at me, I would hold it out in front of me; but just at the time he was not far from me I saw that he cast the sword from him and went his way; and as I wondered thereat, I observed that one went before me who held his sword by the point, and would hand it to him, and give himself up for grace or not grace, which was the reason that he reversed his sword.

June 15-16. The 16th was a Sunday.

[204] There was brought to me a representation of my former life, and of how I have since gone where there were abysses on all sides, and of how I turned about. Then I came into a very glorious grove, filled everywhere with the finest fig trees in splendid growth and order. It seemed that there were some withered figs still left on one. The grove was surrounded with ditches; though there was nothing on the side where I was. I wanted to go over a little bridge, which consisted of high earth with grass upon it; but I did not venture it because of the danger. **[205]** A little way from this I saw a large and very beautiful palace with wings, and I wished to lodge in it because I realized I should then have the prospect of the grove and the ditches. A window a long way down the wing was open. There, I thought, is the room I shall have. It means that on Sunday I shall continue in the spiritual, which is signified by the glorious grove. The palace may be my design for my work, which points to the grove, where I intend to look.

[June] 20-21.

[206] It seemed to me it was deliberated whether or not I should be admitted to the society there, or to any of their councils. My father came out, and told me that what I had written about providence was most beautiful. I remembered that it was only a little treatise.[69] After this one night I was found in the church, but naked,[70] with nothing but my shirt on, so that I did not venture forth. This dream

---

[69]The work mentioned was never published. See Tafel *Doc.* I, p. 585, for list of proposed treatises.

[70]See *The New Church Magazine*, Feb. 1914, p. 80, Tafel *Doc.* II, p. 597, and *New Church Life*, April 1914.

perhaps may mean that I am not yet at all clad and prepared as I ought to be.

[June] 26-27.

[207] I was in a place with many persons. I went past my garden, which had a very poor appearance; this without doubt was in comparison with the heavenly garden. Then I heard afar off persons that were firing cannons against the enemy; firing lengthwise and crosswise; it was represented to me that the enemy was slain. Word was also brought that the Danes were attacking with 10,000 men; it was a sword fight hand to hand; the enemy was completely slain. Then I was in another place, and wished to go out and visit the battlefields. There were many where I was who wished to make their escape, because they were of the Danish party; but I advised them to stay where they were because they had nothing to fear; except one Danish soldier. **[208]** Saw afterwards as it were a great screen which protected me. Saw that I was maimed in the left foot, which I had known nothing of; it was bandaged, but it will soon be all right again. A little bird in a large cage that had been concealed a long time was still alive and had food and drink and went in and out of the cage. Saw Eric Benzelius[71] with a wig with two locks behind; he walked weary and old; followed him, and saw that he went into a church and sat down in the lowest seat.

July 1-2.

[209] Something very wonderful happened to me.[72] I came into strong shudderings, as when Christ showed me the divine grace; one followed the other, ten or fifteen in number. I waited in expectation of being thrown upon my face as the former time, but this did not occur. With the last shudder I was lifted up and with my hands I felt a back. I laid hold of the whole back, as well as put my hands under to the breast in front. Straightway it laid itself down, and I saw in front the countenance also, but this very obscurely. I was then kneeling and thought to myself whether or not I should lay myself down alongside, but this did not occur; it seemed as if it were not permitted. The shudders all started from below in the body and went up to the

---

[71]Eric Benzelius (1675-1743) was librarian of Uppsala University, 1702; professor of theology, 1723; bishop of Gothenburg, 1726; bishop of Linköping, 1731; archbishop of Sweden, 1742. He married Swedenborg's sister Anna in 1703, and became Emanuel's "guide, philosopher and friend."

[72]See the posthumous work, *The Five Senses*, n. 592, text and note.

head. **[210]** This was in a vision when I was neither waking nor sleeping, for I had all my thoughts together. It was the inward man separated from the outward that knew this. When I was quite awake, similar shudders came over me several times. It must have been a holy angel, because I was not thrown on my face. What it could mean our Lord knows best. It seemed that it was told me in the first instance that I should have something for my guidance; or some such thing. God's grace is shown to the inward and outward man in me. To God alone be praise and honor.

[211] From what follows after and on other grounds I notice that it must mean that I shall light upon truths concerning the internal sensations; but touch them upon the back and obscurely in the front. Because, before it came, it seemed it was told me it was an annunciation of that which I have hitherto worked out on this subject, just as it was afterwards shown to me that I was privileged to exchange my poor stivers into better coin; then some little gold was given me; which however still had copper beside it.

July 3-4.

[212] Seemed to take leave of her with particular tenderness, kissing. When another appeared a short way off; the effect while I was awaking was as if I was in continual amorous desire. Yet it was said and as it were complained that it was not at all understood. Which signifies that an end has now come to what I have written on the senses in general,[73] and the operation of the interior faculties, which, as it is projected, cannot be comprehended; and that I am now coming to the second part, on the cerebrum.

July 7-8.

[213] Saw how an oblong globe condensed itself to its highest part from the bottom of the globe; taking the form of a tongue; which then afterwards spread and spread out. Signifies, as I believe, that the innermost was the sanctuary, and served as a center of the lower globe; and that this thing in great part shall be thought out, as the tongue manifested. Believe that I am destined to this; which was unquestionably the signification of the sanctuary I had to do with: as is corroborated by this, that all the objects of the sciences presented themselves to me in the form of women. Furthermore, that it was deliberated, whether I should be admitted into the society where my father was.

[214] Came also upon the sure thoughts, that God's Son is love, who, to do good to the human race, took upon himself their sins; yea, to the very

---

[73]Referring to the work then in progress.

hardest punishment. For if justice existed, mercy must be effected through love.

[July] 9-10.

[215] Was with and conversed with the king, who was afterwards in a room; talked afterwards with his princes with whom I had become acquainted. They conversed among themselves about me. I told them that I am timid in love and veneration. When I wanted to go away, I saw that the queen's table was made ready. I was not clad as I ought to be; for now, as on other occasions, I had hastily put off my white jacket; and I wished to go up and put it on. Spoke with my father, who kissed me because I reminded him not to swear at all. With this, up came the queen with her attendants. It signifies that I enter into acquaintanceship with God's children; for the day before I selected another lodging.[74]

---

[74]After leaving Brockmer's he moved to the house of Richard Shearsmith. (It was here that he died on March 29, 1772.) See Tafel *Doc.* II, p. 599.

[July] 14-15.

[216] Talked with Brita Behm,[75] who it seemed gave birth to a son, but as the husband had long been dead, I wondered how this could be; the child however died. In its place were both Rosenadlers.[76] She took me into a splendid and large carriage of surpassing magnificence and brought me to Count Horn;[77] **[217]** where entertainment was set out. I went away; wished to come there afterwards; flew along, but came to a fine city, which I saw. Noted that I was flying astray and turned about. Signifies my work on the internal senses and the cerebrum which is analogized in Brita Behm's child. The going in a splendid carriage to Count Horn, president in the chancellor's college and primate of the kingdom; going to another town; signifies perhaps being too far away from the soul.

---

[75]Brita Behm (1670-1753) was the younger sister of Swedenborg's mother. In 1684 she married Johan Schwede, who died in 1697. By inheritance she became joint owner with Swedenborg of mining property in Helsingland. See Tafel *Doc.* I, p. 659.

[76]Johan Adrian and Carl Albrecht, the sons of Johan Rosenadler, one of Swedenborg's teachers at Uppsala.

[77]Count Arvid Bernhard Horn (1664-1742) was an eminent Swedish warrior and statesman. He provided leadership after the death of Charles XII, becoming president of the court of chancery in 1726 and prime minister from 1727 to 1738.

[218] Went on a bridge over water; a ship alongside; came to a pit. Thought then about bread, that every day bread more or less was carried thither. May possibly mean the Lutheran body. Christ is likened to spiritual bread.

[July] 21-22.

[219] Saw a congregation in which the members one and all had little crowns on their heads; two stood foremost, with very big and glorious crowns. One of them talked with joy; half in French and half in German. They that had the crowns signified martyrs, of whom I had been thinking the day before; but who the two were and whether one of them was Huss,[78] I am not aware.

[220] A little child insisted on caressing me; drew me to him; but it seemed at last I forbid him. Signified that *a man must be as a child to our Lord;* on which thoughts I afterwards fell; because children have now twice represented themselves; so also the night before. That is, that man is not himself to take so much care about the spiritual, as if it came through his own strength nor yet about the worldly; but as a child cast all anxiety upon our Lord.

---

[78]John Huss, hero of the Moravians, was martyred at Constance in 1415.

[221] Pushed my way into an assembly; thought to go out in time; but all was full; made my way forth however; came upon an empty bench that had a cloth upon it, with which I wanted to cover myself. *Signifies that I by my own pains wanted to enter into the congregation, and also that I wished to preserve myself incognito from others:* which indeed I had done the day before; but the cares ought to be cast on our Lord.

[222] When I wakened, I entered into a vision, wherein I saw much gold before me, and the air full. *Signifies that our Lord, who disposes all, gives me for my spiritual and worldly estates all that I have need of when I as a child cast my cares upon him.*

[July] 22-23.

[223] Seemed to myself to take a very high flying course, but in such a circle that I came down duly when I was tired. Saw a beautiful hall with splendid tapestry covering the walls, all of one piece. It signified that *the day before I had it in my mind and heart, that the all in all is to allow Christ to draw his providing care about us in the spiritual and the worldly.*

[224] Saw that a boy ran away with a shirt of mine and I ran after him. *May mean that I had not washed my feet.*

[July] 24-25.

[225] Besides much else, it seemed that I was in company with many, and we made ourselves merry. It appeared that I was to be the guest of one man. Came away from there to travel; seemed to intend to come back; but when I went, I went away from there, which I had never thought of doing. There met me one that told me that he had cut curtains to my bed; but said something against my science. *Whether I shall take another way with my work, and whether it is in preparation for something else, I am not at all aware.* This is dark to me.

[July] 27-28 [changed from 28-29].

[226] Saw my father in a beautiful garment in front of a congregation; he talked with me in a friendly manner and wished to take me to a person in an inner room who appeared to be asleep and to be telling of me. I went slowly away, being afraid of waking him up. *Means that I then began to read the Bible in the evening, and that I was afraid on Saturday afternoon that I had not prepared myself as I ought.*

[July] 29-30.

[227] Saw a great beast with wings; sometimes it had the appearance of a man but with a great gaping mouth. He did not dare to touch me. I went after him with my sword. Had no chance and no power in my arms of striking him. At last I saw him standing before me with a gun, and he shot out of it some sort of poison, which however did not harm me at all for I was protected. Then immediately after that I stuck the sword down his throat; yet with no great force. I went higher up; and it seemed it was said that he was killed. *The day before I had been thinking of the woman and the dragon in the Apocalypse, and I wished that I could be the instrument to slay the dragon; which thing however stands not in my power but only in God's.*

July 30 - August 1.

[228] Was long in holy shudders; yet at the same time in a deep sleep. Thought whether anything holy was about to appear. Seemed to me as if I was cast upon my face; but cannot certify this. Afterwards was taken away from there and found under my back one who it seemed was an acquaintance. Was annoyed that he had taken me from it [the vision]. Said also, when he was leaving me, that he was not to do so any more. The shudderings afterwards continued; but saw nothing further. It meant that the holy came to me and so moved me that I was carried to my work which I had begun to write today, about the senses;[79] and that I am desirous that it should not draw me away from that which is more important.

[229] Afterwards I waited in expectation of a procession of horses, and some big beautiful light yellow horses came in great numbers; afterwards more, with beautiful teams of horses, which came to me; fat, large, beautiful, adorned with beautiful trappings. Which signifies my work I have now begun; the latter teams, that on the cerebrum, so that I now find that I have God's permission to proceed, and I believe He will help me therein.

August 4-5.

[230] Saw a man come against me with a drawn sword: I seemed also to have a sword with a silver hilt; but when he came, I had nothing except a broken sheath. He lay about on my back, and bit my hands. I cried for help, but none was found.

[231] Afterwards I had to do with a whore in Assessor Brenner's[80] presence; it seemed that I

---

[79]See Tafel *Doc.* I, p. 203.

[80]The original has only "As. B." Elias Brenner (1647-1717), a Swedish archeologist, married Sophia Weber in 1670. See Tafel *Doc.* II, p. 1265.

boasted of the fact that I was so strong. *Signifies, that I was wrong with my God, daily with thoughts that hung by me; and from which no man but God alone can help me; also that I had boasted to D. H. about my work.* I planned the day after to go to God's table, but found from this that no man, but God alone, can forgive sins. I therefore abstained. I thus have been given ground for observation on the subject of confession.

[August] 8-9.

[232] Came to Sweden; saw the kingdom parted into two kingdoms: the larger was on the side of Upland; the other toward Örebro. Two kings: the latter, the lesser; yet the kingdom was said to reach to Bohus. I was with this king, and the kingdom extended itself. It seemed I had a commission as secretary, in Java; but I was found of no use for this service because I did not know the language. Still, I was present. Dreamt afterwards of small birds that sat around the head that should be plucked off. *Signified, that I had not rightly arranged and carried out the subject of the corpus reticulare Malpighii.*[81]

---

[81]See *Regnum Animale*, part III, nn. 495-499.

August 26-27.

[233] The previous days I was much troubled and as it were burdened with my sins, which it seemed to me were not forgiven me, which hindered me the last time from partaking of the Lord's Supper. Then I seemed the day before to be lightened. In the night it seemed that the soles of the foot were quite white, *which means that my sins are forgiven;* also means much more, that I am once more welcome again.

[August] 27-28.

[234] I seemed to take a book from my father's library. Sat afterwards in a ship. Sat with another where the helm usually is. On the right hand was another. When I stood up, another sat in my place; yes, and when I wished to resume it, he moved his seat higher up and gave me room. A woman sat on the left side; in front of me sat another. I rose up, and let her sit there. She sat down, but now there was no easy chair, but only a straight chair, and I was then in front. **[235]** Wine, apparently cowslip wine, was being served in a large drinking mug; one was given to me, and I emptied it in one gulp. It was the most delicious I had ever tasted. Came to me without any thought that it seemed to be a heavenly nectar. A man sat always in his place at the top beside the rudder. *Signifies, how I get help in my work from a higher hand, so that I am only* *used as an instrument.* Wherefore I also had in attendance with me one whose business I said it was to sweep clean. This signifies me also.

August 1-2 [September].

[236] Intended on the second of August [September] to go to God's table because I am assured, according to my knowledge, that I am rescued from my sins. But then I saw a big dog that ran to me but did me no harm. I showed him to another that sat beside me, to whom also he did no harm. It signifies either that the day before I chose to boast of one of my visits or that the others flatter me.

[237] Afterwards it seemed I perceived that Didron[82] went away from his king, with whom he was in such high favor, and betook himself to the Danes, and there died; and that his wife, who was false, was the cause of this, and waited for his dead body. *Hear now at once, as he also inspired me, that I ought by no means to depart from the congregation of Christ; and thither to take the Lord's Supper; and that in this case I become spiritually dead again.* I could not understand anything further; there is therefore a mystery underneath this. I refrained myself therefrom; was kindled by the Holy Spirit, as

---

[82]John Fredrik Didron (1686-1747) was a Swedish courtier, soldier and politician, a friend of King Fredrik I, and an active leader of the "Caps." See Note 39 above.

often happens when I dispose myself according to command.

September 16. Sunday after dinner.

[238] In the night between the 15th and 16th, I saw in my sleep two kings, the king of France and the king of Poland, who proposed sublime things; afterwards a little girl, who sang for me when I went out. *Signified that what I had written met with approval, which was the last part of the first chapter on the sense of touch.*[83]

[239] Immediately after dinner, when I was asleep, a woman was presented to me, but I did not see her face; she was very stout; in very white clothes. I wanted to buy something of her to drink. She said she had nothing left; but there was one beside her who gave me his right to get a glass which she had hidden in her clothes. When she looked for it, I saw how very stout she was, like a woman with child. After looking in the folds of her sleeve, she recovered again what she had for a drink; thought it was chocolate; but it was wine. I did not want to have it as it was chocolate; but just then I awoke. It seemed to me then as also on one or two occasions before that I had a pretty strong consciousness of the smell of wine. I wondered

---

[83]In Part III, *Regnum Animale.*

especially at her snow white clothes. *I cannot well say what this means* whether or not it was the woman *I had when the word "sanctuary" was mentioned,*[84] *for I did not now see the face, and moreover she was with child; which may signify that I am now in fact rightly writing and producing what I have in view. For that day I found myself greatly enlightened in those things that I had in hand.*

[September] 17-18.

[240] Saw the king of Prussia, and one that said he was going away to sow enmity between the kings of Prussia and France.

[September] 18-19.

[241] It seemed to me I went over ground which was particularly rugged; went with an iron stick in my hand, which thereafter was not at all heavy to walk with. Came to the end of the same ground. Lay in a bed. There came against me a very large ox, black, with horns, which seemed as if it would gore me. I was frightened, but it was said to me, "You shall go through it safely." *Wakened. Something awaits me when I have gone through the first chapter on the sense of touch.*

---

[84]See n. 171, above.

[September] 21 [changed from 27].

[242] It was a Sunday. Before I slept I was in deep thought on the subject about which I am writing. Then it was said to me, "Hold your tongue," or "I will strike you." Then I saw a person sitting upon some ice, and I was afraid. I was as in a vision; I kept in my thoughts and experienced the usual shuddering, which implied that I ought not to work so long, particularly on Sunday; or perhaps in the evenings.

[September] 29-30.

[243] This was from Saturday till Sunday. I saw a gable of the most beautiful palace that could possibly be seen; glory like the sun upon it. It was said to me that in the society it was decided that I should be a member that was immortal, which no one previously had been except one who had been dead and had lived again. Others said that there were several. I wondered if it were not more important to be with God and so to live. *This referred to that which I have now brought to an end about organic forms in general, and chiefly the end.*[85] **[244]** Afterwards a person said that he would call upon

---

[85]The end of this chapter of *Regnum Animale* deals with the mind's ability to distinguish between what is good and useful and what is vile and useless.

me at 10:00 o'clock. He did not know where I lived. I answered then as I thought that I lived in the gable of the palace; which meant that that *which with God's help I have written lately about forms*[86] *is such that it shall carry me on still further to that which is still more glorious.*

[245] Afterwards I was with women but would not touch them as I had previously had to do with that which was holy; wherewith much occurred to me which I left to God's good pleasure. Because I am as an instrument with which he does according to his pleasure; yet would wish to be with the aforesaid. Yet not my will but God's. God grant that herein I do not err. I believe I do not.

October 3. After dinner.

[246] I fell into a short sleep. It was represented how all is inmostly in unities; the rationale of the cause [*ratio causae*], the end; whence our thoughts considered in this light as unities bear within them no other end and reason than that which comes into them from the Spirit of God, or the spirit of the body; if from the body, then all is sin from the innermost; for we aim after nothing else than that which strives against the spiritual. Which rules we

---

[86]See *The Five Senses*, nn. 262-291.

ourselves may observe if we reflect from our loves, which in fact accompany.

[October] 3 to 6.

[247] Several times I have remarked that there are spirits of all descriptions. The one spirit which is Christ's is the only spirit which has all blessedness with it. By the others man is enticed in a thousand ways to go in with them; but unhappy is he that does so. There came before me time after time Korah and Dathan[87] who brought strange fire upon the altar, and it had no power to save. So it is when any other fire is brought in than that which comes from Christ. I saw also as it were a fire that came to me. Therefore it is necessary to discern the spirits, which is a thing man cannot do except through Christ himself and His Spirit.

[248] The horrible danger in which I had been on the night between the 29th and 30th[88] was represented to me afterwards in my sleep, when I was on a piece of ice which could hardly bear me, and I came next to a hideous great gulf. A person on the other side was unable to come to help me, for I walked backwards. But God through Christ is the only one that helped me herein. He is my Lord and

---

[87]See the Book of Numbers 16.

[88]The correct date was Sept. 21.

Master, and I am his slave. Honor and thanks to him, without whom no one can come to God.

October 6-7.

[249] It was very much and yet very merciful. How a black veil or skin which was drawn over, shining, yet had no substance; it was said that it would not keep right, for it was crumpled together. And it was promised to enlighten me better; there was seen also as it were an inward light. I wish myself to do it on Sundays: *Meaning that I had gone with my understanding and fantasy into something, which is analogous to the black gauze which does not keep right. Again I saw an abyss which is the danger I am in with my thoughts.* **[250]** Otherwise, it is something told me about my book. One said that it was a divine book on the *Worship and Love of God.*[89] I believe it was also something about spirits. I believed I had something about this in my book on *The Infinite.*[90] But to this no answer was made. I came afterwards into the thoughts and into the information, that *all love to anything whatever, for instance to my works I have in hand; when one loves them and not as a medium to the only love that is to God and Christ Jesus, is a meretricious love.*

---

[89]Published by Swedenborg in London in 1745.

[90]Published by Swedenborg in 1734.

Wherefore also such things *are likened always to whoredom in God's Word. This is also that which has befallen me.* But when *a man has love for God the foremost of all, then he has thereto no other love, than that which he finds by this means will advance the love of God.* **[251]** I thought I also saw Czar Peter and other great emperors, who despised me because I had half sleeves. I do not know whose retinue they belong to. Several times beautiful bread and other things had been given me. *God grant that it is as I believe the spiritual bread.*

[252] From this and the foregoing we find how soon and how easily a human being is deceived by other spirits, *which represent themselves according to the love of each and every person, for loves are represented by spirits,* indeed in very fact by women.

[October] 7-8.

[253] It seemed to me that I wanted to go along a road but saw a little boy going up a little path. I followed him, but there was a mist. It seemed that there were soldiers near by. I walked crouching and afraid. Yet it seemed to me they were not enemies but some of our own people. But I found that I could not see any way out. Turned around and came into a disordered place. Asked for another room; got one. Asked for water. He said it was fresh and muddy. Therefore asked for milk. Wakened. *Means that I had been on the wrong road and* *followed my own understanding in a mist; a time when a man is frightened even of his own people as if they were enemies. But when a man goes the right way, he is afraid of nobody. The water means that it is still muddied: milk, that it ought to be strengthened still more.*

[254] Saw afterwards in vision one that had a black cloak, but it was taken away, and he disappeared. *Means that the former black veil disappeared. When a man goes only in such a way that he trusts in God and Christ alone, and in nowise in himself, or sets his own understanding hand to hand against self, then he finds that we are soldiers fighting against satan continually. When a man has God's spirit and life, then is it daily a victory. But in the other case it is daily a destruction; such a man falls from one defeat into another. Thus a man ought never to despair but trust in the grace of God.* **[255]** The night before it seemed I saw [was offered] a commission as a captain, lieutenant, or something of the sort; but I sought out Secretary Bierchenius[91] to tell him that I wished to remain in my former post as assessor; which meant that I did not then understand what was implied by being a soldier and fighting against satan; for God sends angels with the soldiers that fight for him. This is the black mantle

---

[91]Hans Bierchenius, secretary of the College of Mines, was one of Swedenborg's associates and friends. See reference to him in *S.D.* n. 4717.

that was drawn aside, and God himself has been pleased to enlighten me in it.

[256] *Saw likewise* in vision a heart full of blood; *it was love.*

[October] 8-9.

[257] This night was the most delightful of all, because I saw the kingdom of innocence. Saw below me the loveliest garden that could be seen. On every tree white roses were set in succession. Went afterwards into a long room. There were beautiful white dishes with milk and bread in them, so appetizing that nothing more appetizing could be imagined. I was in company with a woman whom I do not remember particularly. **[258]** Then I went back. A pretty little innocent child came to me and told me that the woman had gone away without taking leave and begged me to buy her a book that she might take up; but showed me nothing. Wakened. Besides this it seemed I entertained on my own account a number of people in a house or palace standing by itself, where there were some acquaintances: among them Senator Lagerberg;[92]

---

[92]Sven Lagerberg (1672-1746) was part of Charles XII government. He became a senator in 1723.

also, I think, Ehrenpreus[93] and others. It was all at my expense. I realized it cost me much, but my thoughts went to and fro about the expense. Meanwhile I did not care about it for I observed that all was maintained by the Lord, who owned the property or showed it me. **[259]** *Was in the kingdom of innocence, and as to my entertaining the other and worldly people without seeing them, does it signify my work, that I should as it were not be with them, although I entertained them therewith; or does it mean something else? The child was innocence itself. I was much moved by it and wished to be in such a kingdom where all is innocence. Lamented that in waking I came away from it. What the woman was that went away without taking leave I am not aware.*

[260] The day after, namely, the 9th, I was so clear-sighted that I was able to read the finely printed Bible without the least difficulty.

[October] 9-10.

[261] Saw in vision a coal fire brightly burning, *which signifies the fire of love.* Afterwards I was in company with women who had teeth on a certain place which I wished to penetrate, but the teeth interfered; *which signified that the day before I had*

---

[93]Count Carl Ehrenpreus (1696-1760) also served under Charles XII. See *S.D.* nn. 5996, 6028.

been busy with my work which is quite different from the other and quite another love if it should prevail, and is not to be regarded as a matter of words or as a plaything in regard to the other. **[262]** When I wakened,I had completely decided to abandon this work; which also would have happened were it not that afterwards in sleep it seemed I was sent to a certain place with a letter. I could not find the way; but my sister Hedwig saw the letter; said it was to Ulrica Adlersteen[94] who was found to have been longing for me for a considerable time. I came there; also saw Schönström. Afterwards continually I had the senses before me; how they go up to the cerebrum, and down. *By this I was strengthened in continuing my work.* **[263]** *God grant that it be not against His good pleasure, which I cannot deduce from the dream without setting myself to the trial of whether I shall abandon the work; to which resolution however God helped me. To God alone be praise and honor.* But a child fell upon my foot and struck itself, and screamed; I wanted to help it up, and asked, "Why do you romp so?" *Means without doubt that I want to rush too quickly in this.*

---

[94]Baroness Ulrika Aldersteen was born in 1694, daughter of Baron Göran Aldersteen. In 1715 she married Albrecht Schönström, son of Peter Swedberg, the brother of Jesper Swedberg. See Tafel *Doc.* I, p. 85.

[October] 10-11.

[264] Seemed as if I was in bed with a woman, but did not touch her. Came afterwards to a gentleman and asked if I could get into his service, because I had lost my post through the war; but he said, "No." They played a kind of *basset*,[95] the coins went back and forth; I was however always with them. I asked my servant if he had said that I owned anything: he said, "No"; said that he should say nothing else. *Signifies the Moravian Church, my being there and not accepted; and my saying that I have no knowledge in religion but have lost it all; and those that play basset win here and there.*

[October] 12-13.

[265] It seemed to me that a person was beaten and scourged, and afterwards above as well as below preached with great earnestness and enforced the same. *Signifies that when a man is chastised by our Lord, the man afterwards gets greater earnestness and spirit to go on in that which the spirit carries him to, so that the chastisement and the punishment make increase therein. I had thought the day before that I was so satisfied that I gave my thoughts a*

---

[95]A card game.

certain free course; the punishment may change this, as a reply to which this came.

[266] Afterwards it seemed to me I said to myself that the Lord himself will inform me: *for as I found, I am in the state of knowing nothing therein, except that Christ ought to be all in all, or God through Christ; so that we cannot ourself do the very least thereto; still less strive; for it is best to give oneself up in surrender at discretion: and still further, could a man therein be quite passive, it were the most perfect.* **[267]** I saw also in vision that fine bread on a plate was presented to me; *which was a sign that the Lord himself will instruct me since I have now come first into the condition that I know nothing, and all preconceived judgments are taken away from me; which is where learning commences: namely, first to be a child and thus be nursed into knowledge, as is the case with me now.*

[October] 13-14.

[268] Among other things it was told me that for the last fourteen days my appearance has been growing much handsomer, and to be like that of an angel. God grant that it be so. God stand by me herein and never take his grace from me.

[October] 15-16.

[269] Saw *in a vision* that a man was under a great burden, and carried loads of wood; fell down under the burden, and another came to his help; but how he was helped I did not see. Saw in my sleep that at length I went up a little bridge, and saw chasms and dangers before me. Afterwards I climbed up by a rope after another person; but saw no end nor how I could arrive at the top. *Signifies that self-centered people who strive to help them-selves to heaven, or to that which is high, labor in vain and with continual danger. Whereas it is easy when a man addresses himself to God, who hath the help in such conditions.*

October 18-19.

[270] Dreamed that a big dog which I thought was chained flew at me and bit me in the leg. Someone came who held his horrible jaws and prevented him from doing any more harm. *Meant that the day before I had heard an oration in the medical college, and I desired in thought that they should name me as the one who understands anatomy best; yet I was glad that it did not happen. The night afterwards I saw someone limping leave me; which may be that through this desire I had become like one lame.*

¶[October] 19-20.

[271] I saw one beast after another; they were spreading out their wings. They were dragons. I flew over them away; but one I hit against. *Such dragons signify spurious loves; which seem as if they are not dragons until one gets to see the wings.* This I had now under hand to write about.

[October] 20-21.

[272] *It was very merciful and remarkable. The day before, I found myself to be unworthy of all the grace God had been pleased to show me because love of self and pride were so deeply rooted in me; prayed God therefore to take them from me because this is not in my own power. Found myself in the evening in a strange situation which I had never before found myself in; that in a manner I despaired of God's grace; though I still knew that God is very gracious, and to me in particular has shown greater grace than to others. It was an anguish in the soul but not in the mind; so that it was not felt otherwise than in the mind itself; without any pain in the body.* **[273]** Thereupon I fell asleep; and saw two dogs that followed close behind me. At last I got rid of them, and it was said to me in thought that this strange pain was to cure me from these. *There is thus such a pain when the root has to be taken away from that* *which is so deeply rooted; which deserves to be very well remembered and kept in the thoughts.*

[274] Afterwards I saw a great king, who was the king of France, who went without a retinue and had such a lowly estate that he could not from that be regarded as a king. One who was with me did not like to acknowledge him as a king. I said that he is such that he does not trouble himself about it. Was polite to all without distinction; talked also with me. When he went out he again had no retinue but took on himself the burdens of others and bore them like clothes. Came therefrom into another great company, where there was much greater state. **[275]** Afterwards I saw the queen: then a chamberlain came and bowed; she likewise made equally deep reverence; there was no pride in her. *Signifies that in Christ dwells not the least pride but that he makes himself equal with others although he is the greatest king; and does not trouble himself about that which is great; moreover, that he takes the burdens of others upon him. The queen, who is wisdom, is like this also and has no self-love and sees herself no higher in herself because she is queen.*

October 26-27.

[276] *It was said to me before that the 27th of October should come again, when I undertook "The Worship and Love of God."* It seemed it was Christ himself with whom I associated as with any other man, without ceremony. He borrowed a little money from another person, some five pfennig. I was sorry that he did not borrow it from me. I took up two [pfennig], of which it seemed I let one drop, *and then another also. He asked what it was. I said* that I have found two; one may have fallen from him. I gave him them and he received them. In such an innocent manner we seemed to live together, which was the state of innocence.

[277] Afterwards I was in my bedroom with another, an acquaintance or kinsman, and told him that I wanted to show him that I lodged better. With this I went out with him first into an adjacent room which extended far on and on, room after room, but did not belong to me. Someone in a bed asked what he wanted. I went out with him into my parlor. When I opened the door, I saw that a whole market place was lodged there and just in front of me a great store of goods. On the other side of that the flank of a large palace; but this was taken down. Then in front and at the sides there seemed to be a place full of beautiful vessels, porcelain as it appeared to me, just set out; at the side all was in process of arrangement. And I afterwards entered into my little room, which also shone. [278] *This signifies all the work I now take in hand in God's name; in front, on "The Worship of God"; at the side, "On Love"; and signifies that I ought not to take any one else's goods, but only my own; as it was in my parlor which I rented; my room also alongside meant*

the other work, and the rooms at the side meant that which did not belong to me. God lead me in the right way. Christ said that I ought not to undertake anything without him.

[279] I sat on a beautiful black horse; there were two of us; he was brave; went first out of the way, but afterwards turned around; meant that which I was to undertake, which still was dark to me but comes right at last.

[280] When I went with my friend through a long passage, a pretty girl came and fell into his arms and as it were sobbed. I asked if she knew him. She did not answer. I took her from him and led her by the arm. *It was my other work to which she addressed herself and from which I took her in this way.*

[281] In the morning in a vision there appeared to me the market called the Disting Fair[96] in my father's house in Upsala in the upstairs parlor, in the entrance and everywhere else in all the upper part. *This signifies the same, showing that it ought to happen with all the more certainty.*

[282] In the morning when I wakened there came upon me again the same kind of giddiness or swoon that I had six or seven years ago in Amsterdam, when I began the *Economy of the Animal Kingdom;*

---

[96]An annual fair and festival held in the city of Uppsala. See Tafel *Doc.* II, p. 218. But see also Mallett's *Northern Antiquities,* p. 549.

but much more subtle; so that I appeared to be near death. It came when I saw the light; threw me upon my face; but passed off by degrees; because little periods of sleep came over me. This swoon then was more inward and deep, but soon passed away. *Signifies, as then, that my head is actually swept and cleansed from that which would hinder these thoughts, as also happened on the former occasion, because it gave me penetration, especially with the pen.* This too was now represented to me in that I seemed to write a fine hand.

[On p. 99 of the manuscript there are only the last four words; several blank pages then intervene following which we find the following notes.]

[May?] 11-13.

[283] It seemed to me that I was with Oelreich and two women; he laid down; and afterwards it seemed he had been with a woman. He admitted it. It occurred to me, as I also stated, that I also had lain with one, and my father saw it, but went past, and said not a word about it.

[284] I walked away from Oelreich and on the way there was deep water, but at the side there was very little. I therefore took the path at the side and thought to myself that I ought not to go into the deep water.

[285] It seemed that a rocket burst over me spreading a number of sparkles of lovely fire. Love for what is high, perhaps.

---

[286][97] Truths or virgins of this sort think it base to be exposed to sale; they regard themselves as so precious and dear to their admirers that they think it an indignity if any one bids for them; still more so if he comes to buy them. Others, who regard them as of no account, they treat superciliously. So then, in order that they may not fall under valuation by the former, nor into contempt from the latter, they prefer to offer themselves gratuitously to their lovers. I, who am their servant, do not dare to disobey them, for fear of being deprived of their service. [The last sentence from *I* is crossed out.]

[97]Odhner notes that this paragraph was written in Latin at the end of the original manuscript. See also nn. 213, 252 above.

INDEX

[The figures refer to paragraph numbers.]